The Glenstal Book of Daily Prayer

'First of all, with instant prayer, beg that He would bring
to completion every good you set out to do.'
Prologue to the Rule of St Benedict

The Glenstal Book of Daily Prayer

A BENEDICTINE PRAYER BOOK

LITURGICAL PRESS
Collegeville, Minnesota

www.litpress.org

Published in North America
by
LITURGICAL PRESS
Collegeville, Minnesota 56321

Designed by Bill Bolger
Origination by The Columba Press
Printed in Canada

ISBN 978-0-8146-3273-4

Acknowledgements

Grateful acknowledgement is made to the following for permission to use copyright material: Biblical quotations are from the *New Revised Standard Version*, copyright © 1989, by the Division of Christian Education of the National Council of the Churches of Christ in the USA, and are used by permission; Psalm Prayers from *Common Worship: Daily Prayer* are copyright © The Archbishops' Council 2005 and are reproduced by permission. Excerpts from the English translation of *The Roman Missal* © 1973, International Committee on English in the Liturgy, Inc. (ICEL), all rights reserved; English translation of the *Benedictus* and the *Magnificat* by the International Consultation on English Texts; Psalm texts from *The Grail Psalms, Inclusive Language Edition*, © 1995 The Grail (England), published by HarperCollins Publishers; Prayers from *Proclaiming All Your Wonders* are used by kind permission of Dominican Publications.

Contents

Introduction

Prayer is our response to God, Father, Son and Holy Spirit, who speaks to us in every moment of our existence. His word reaches us in many and various ways: through the created world of nature, through the great religions and their holy books, and through the multitude of people who touch our lives for better or for worse. All are ways in which the living God communicates with us. But Christians believe that God speaks most fully in the person and work of Jesus Christ his Son and Word, whom he sent into the world to redeem us and lead us to himself. Jesus, God's Word-made-flesh, is the light that helps us find the face of God, the path we must follow if we are to grow into likeness with God himself, the vocation of all human beings.

In prayer we make our response of thanksgiving and praise, acknowledging God's goodness. In addition, we bring the needs of the whole world, and of all who suffer, before God's face asking for his mercy and confiding them to his care. This is done in union with the great family of witnesses who have heard God's voice and responded to his will throughout the ages: Mary the mother of Jesus and the angels and saints.

In Christian tradition, the two most cherished times for prayer are in the morning (Lauds) and in the evening (Vespers). In morning prayer we consecrate the day to God, recalling and celebrating the light of Christ who visits us like the dawn from on high; in the evening, remembering that Christ's light will never die, we give thanks for the day that is past.

Monastic tradition has added through the centuries four other times, called in this book 'prayer-stops', at which we remember the coming of the Holy Spirit, Christ's crucifixion and his burial. They are an opportunity in the course of the day to remember God's presence and the great things he has done for the world in Christ. The final one is the beautiful office of Compline, in which we commend ourselves to God's protection before we go to sleep.

The major part of this book is composed of Psalms, each with an added Psalm-prayer at the end. The Psalm-prayers pick up and elaborate for private prayer some of the main themes found in the Psalm that has been said.

In this prayer book, again reflecting the monastic tradition, we have placed special emphasis on the role of the body and on the importance of symbolism in prayer, suggesting the use of gestures such as bowing and symbols such as light and incense. Human beings are embodied people and the body too must play its part in our relationship with God.

We hope that some of the riches of the Benedictine monastic vision might be shared once more with those who use this book, 'that in all things God may receive the glory.'

Morning and Evening Prayer:
Lauds and Vespers

Week 1 Sunday Morning: Lauds

The Sign of the Cross is traced on the lips while the opening verse is said.

O Lord, open my lips.
And my mouth shall praise your name.

Glory be to the Father, and to the Son, and to the Holy Spirit: as it was in the beginning, is now, and ever shall be, world without end. Amen. (Alleluia.)

A candle may be lit in front of a Cross, a Bible, an icon or a statue during the invocation of the light.

Glory be to God who has shown us the light!
Lead me from darkness to light.
Lead me from sadness to joy.
Lead me from death to immortality.
Glory be to God who has shown us the light!

A deep bow or other gesture of reverence may be made while the following psalm verses are said:

Come, ring out our joy to the Lord;
hail the rock who saves us.

O that today you would listen to God's voice!
'Harden not your hearts'.

Glory be to the Father... (Ps 95:1, 7b, 8a)

Psalm

(Alleluia!)
Give thanks to the Lord who is good,
for God's love endures for ever.

The stone which the builders rejected
has become the corner stone.
This is the work of the Lord,
a marvel in our eyes.
This day was made by the Lord;
we rejoice and are glad.

O Lord, grant us salvation;
O Lord, grant success.
Blessed in the name of the Lord is he who comes.
We bless you from the house of the Lord;
the Lord God is our light.

Go forward in procession with branches
even to the altar.
You are my God, I thank you.
My God, I praise you.
Give thanks to the Lord who is good;
for God's love endures for ever.

Glory be to the Father... (Ps 118:1, 22-29)

Psalm Prayer
Saving God,
open the gates of righteousness,
that your pilgrim people may enter and be built into a living
temple on the cornerstone of our salvation,
Jesus Christ our Lord. Amen.

Canticle
Blessed are you, O Lord, God of our ancestors,
and to be praised and highly exalted for ever;

And blessed is your glorious, holy name,
and to be highly praised and highly exalted for ever.

Blessed are you in the temple of your holy glory,
and to be extolled and highly glorified for ever.

Blessed are you who look into the depths from your
throne on the cherubim,
and to be praised and highly exalted for ever.

Blessed are you on the throne of your kingdom,
and to be extolled and highly exalted for ever.

Blessed are you in the firmament of heaven,
and to be sung and glorified for ever.

Glory be to the Father... (Dan 3:52-57)

Psalm of Praise
(Alleluia!)
Praise the Lord from the heavens,
praise God in the heights.
Praise God, all you angels,
praise him, all you hosts.

Praise God, sun and moon,
praise him, shining stars.
Praise God, highest heavens
and the waters above the heavens.

Let them praise the name of the Lord.
The Lord commanded: they were made.
God fixed them forever,
gave a law which shall not pass away.

God exalts the strength of the people,
is the praise of all the saints,
of the sons and daughters of Israel,
of the people to whom he comes close.
(Alleluia!)

Glory be to the Father... (Ps 148:1-6, 14)

Psalm Prayer
O glorious God,
your whole creation sings your marvellous work;
may heaven's praise so echo in our hearts
that we may be good stewards of the earth;
through Jesus Christ our Lord. Amen.

Scripture reading

If you have been raised with Christ, seek the things that
are above, where Christ is, seated at the right hand of
God. Set your minds on things that are above, not on
things that are on earth, for you have died, and your life is
hidden with Christ in God. When Christ who is your life
is revealed, then you also will be revealed with him in
glory. (Col 3:1-4)

The reading is followed by a pause for silent reflection.

The Sign of the Cross is made at the beginning of the
Gospel Canticle.

Gospel Canticle – The Benedictus

Blessed be the Lord, the God of Israel;
he has come to his people and set them free.
He has raised up for us a mighty saviour,
born of the house of his servant David.

Through his holy prophets he promised of old
that he would save us from our enemies,
from the hands of all who hate us.
He promised to show mercy to our fathers
and to remember his holy covenant.

This was the oath he swore to our father Abraham:
to set us free from the hands of our enemies,
free to worship him without fear,
holy and righteous in his sight all the days of our life.
You, my child, shall be called the prophet of the Most High

for you will go before the Lord to prepare his way,
to give his people knowledge of salvation
by forgiving them their sins.

In the tender compassion of our God
the dawn from on high shall break upon us,
to shine on those who dwell in darkness
and the shadow of death,
and to guide our feet on the road of peace.

Glory be to the Father ... (Lk 1:68-79)

Silent thanksgiving is made for the following:
For the promise of eternity in Christ's resurrection from
the dead ...
For the new life received in baptism ...
For the fruitfulness of creation ...

During the Lord's Prayer the hands may be opened and
extended.

Our Father, who art in heaven,
hallowed be thy name.
Thy kingdom come.
Thy will be done on earth as it is in heaven.
Give us this day our daily bread,
and forgive us our trespasses
as we forgive those who trespass against us,
and lead us not into temptation,
but deliver us from evil.

Concluding Prayer
Father of mercy,
your love embraces everyone
and through the resurrection of your Son
you call us into your wonderful light.
Dispel our darkness
and make us a people with one heart and one voice,
forever singing your praise,
in Jesus, the Christ, our Lord. Amen.

The Sign of the Cross is made as the Blessing is said.

May Christ our Lord, by the power of his resurrection
have mercy on us and save us. Amen.

To the holy and undivided Trinity,
to the Father of all good gifts,
to the humanity of our Lord Jesus Christ, crucified and risen,
be all praise, honour and adoration
at this time and forevermore.

May the souls of the faithful departed through the mercy
of God rest in peace. Amen.

Week 1 Sunday Evening: Vespers

The Sign of the Cross is made while the opening verse is said.

O God, come to my assistance.
O Lord, make haste to help me.

Glory be to the Father, and to the Son, and to the Holy Spirit: as it was in the beginning, is now, and ever shall be, world without end. Amen. (Alleluia.)

A candle may be lit in front of a Cross, a Bible, an icon or a statue during the thanksgiving for the light.

O joyful light of the holy glory of the Immortal Father,
heavenly, holy, blessed Jesus Christ!
Now that we have come to the sun's hour of rest,
the lights of evening round us shine.
We praise the Father, the Son and the Holy Spirit, One God.
Worthy are you, O Lord,
at all times to be praised with undefiled tongue,
O Son of God, O giver of life!
Therefore you are glorified throughout the universe.

Incense may be burned while the following psalm verses are said:

Let my prayer arise before you like incense,
the raising of my hands like an evening sacrifice.

I have called to you, Lord; hasten to help me!
Hear my prayer when I cry to you!

Glory be to the Father... (Ps 141:2, 1)

Psalm
(Alleluia!)
When Israel came forth from Egypt,
Jacob's family from an alien people,
Judah became the Lord's temple,
Israel became God's kingdom.

The sea fled at the sight,
the Jordan turned back on its course,
the mountains leapt like rams
and the hills like yearling sheep.

Why was it, sea, that you fled,
that you turned back, Jordan, on your course?
Mountains, that you leapt like rams;
hills, like yearling sheep?

Tremble, O earth, before the Lord,
in the presence of the God of Jacob,
who turns the rock into a pool
and flint into a spring of water.

Glory be to the Father ... (Ps 114)

Psalm Prayer

Strike the rock of our hard hearts, O God,
and let our tears of joy and sorrow
mould us to bear the imprint of your love,
given in Christ our risen Lord. Amen.

Canticle

(Alleluia!)
Salvation and glory and power to our God!

Praise our God, all you his servants,
and all who fear him, small and great.

For the Lord our God, the Almighty, reigns.
Let us rejoice and exult and give him the glory.

For the marriage of the Lamb has come,
and his bride has made herself ready.

Blessed are those who are invited
to the marriage supper of the Lamb.

Glory be to the Father … (Rev 19:1b, 5b, 6b, 7, 9b)

Psalm of Praise

(Alleluia!)
My soul, give praise to the Lord;
I will praise the Lord all my days,
make music to my God while I live.

It is the Lord who keeps faith for ever,
who is just to those who are oppressed.
It is God who gives bread to the hungry,
the Lord who sets prisoners free,

the Lord who gives sight to the blind,
who raises up those who are bowed down,
the Lord, who protects the stranger
and upholds the widow and orphan.

It is the Lord who loves the just
but thwarts the path of the wicked.
The Lord will reign for ever,
Zion's God, from age to age.
(Alleluia!)

Glory be to the Father ... (Ps 146:1-2, 6b-9)

Psalm Prayer
Lord of all,
our breath and being come from you,
yet our earthly end is dust;
as you loose the bound and feed the hungry,
so bring us in your mercy
through the grave and gate of death
to the feast of eternal life,
where you reign for evermore. Amen.

Scripture reading
Do not be afraid; I am the first and the last, and the living
one. I was dead, and see, I am alive for ever and ever; and
I have the keys of Death and of Hades. (Rev 1:17c-18)

The reading is followed by a pause for silent reflection.

The Sign of the Cross is made at the beginning of the Gospel Canticle. Incense may be burned.

Gospel Canticle – The Magnificat
My soul proclaims the greatness of the Lord,
my spirit rejoices in God my Saviour;
for he has looked with favour on his lowly servant,
and from this day all generations will call me blessed.

The Almighty has done great things for me:
holy is his Name.
He has mercy on those who fear him
in every generation.

He has shown the strength of his arm,
he has scattered the proud in their conceit.
He has cast down the mighty from their thrones,
and has lifted up the lowly.
He has filled the hungry with good things,
and has sent the rich away empty.

He has come to the help of his servant Israel
for he has remembered his promise of mercy,
the promise he made to our fathers,
to Abraham and his children for ever.

Glory be to the Father … (Lk 1:46-55)

Silent intercession is made for the following intentions:

For the mission and ministry of the Church …

For friends, relations and neighbours …

For all in any kind of need …

During the Lord's Prayer the hands may be opened and extended.

Our Father, who art in heaven,
hallowed be thy name.
Thy kingdom come.
Thy will be done on earth as it is in heaven.
Give us this day our daily bread,
and forgive us our trespasses
as we forgive those who trespass against us,
and lead us not into temptation,
but deliver us from evil.

Concluding Prayer

We give you thanks, Lord our God,
for this day, now drawing to a close.
May our prayer, rising before you like incense,
be pleasing to you;
and may our outstretched hands
be filled with your mercy,
through Jesus, your Son, our Lord. Amen.

The Sign of the Cross is made as the Blessing is said.

May Christ our Lord, by the power of his resurrection
have mercy on us and save us. Amen.

To the holy and undivided Trinity,
to the Father of all good gifts,
to the humanity of our Lord Jesus Christ, crucified and risen,
be all praise, honour and adoration
at this time and forevermore.

May the souls of the faithful departed through the mercy
of God rest in peace. Amen.

Week 1 Monday Morning: Lauds

O Lord, open my lips.
And my mouth shall praise your name.

Glory be to the Father, and to the Son, and to the Holy Spirit: as it was in the beginning, is now, and ever shall be, world without end. Amen. (Alleluia.)

Glory be to God who has shown us the light!
Lead me from darkness to light.
Lead me from sadness to joy.
Lead me from death to immortality.
Glory be to God who has shown us the light!

Come, ring out our joy to the Lord;
hail the rock who saves us.

O that today you would listen to God's voice!
'Harden not your hearts'.

Glory be to the Father... (Ps 95:1, 7b, 8a)

Psalm

The heavens proclaim the glory of God,
and the firmament shows forth the work of God's hands.
Day unto day takes up the story
and night unto night makes known the message.

No speech, no word, no voice is heard
yet their span extends through all the earth,
their words to the utmost bounds of the world.

There God has placed a tent for the sun;
it comes forth like a bridegroom coming from his tent,
rejoices like a champion to run its course.

At the end of the sky is the rising of the sun;
to the furthest end of the sky is its course.
There is nothing concealed from its burning heat.

Glory be to the Father … (Ps 19:1-7)

Psalm Prayer

Christ, the sun of righteousness,
rise in our hearts this day,
enfold us in the brightness of your love
and bear us at the last to heaven's horizon;
for your love's sake. Amen.

Canticle

Blessed are you, O Lord, the God of our ancestor Israel,
for ever and ever.
Yours, O Lord, are the greatness, the power, the glory,
the victory, and the majesty;
for all that is in the heavens and on the earth is yours;
yours is the kingdom, O Lord,
and you are exalted as head above all.

Riches and honour come from you,
and you rule over all.
In your hand are power and might;
and it is in your hand to make great
and to give strength to all.

And now, our God, we give thanks to you
and praise your glorious name.
For all things come from you,
and of your own have we given you.

Glory be to the Father ... (1 Chron 29:10b-13, 14b)

Psalm of Praise

(Alleluia!)
Praise the Lord from the heavens,
praise God in the heights.
Praise God, all you angels,
praise him, all you hosts.

Praise God, sun and moon,
praise him, shining stars.
Praise God, highest heavens
and the waters above the heavens.

Let them praise the name of the Lord.
The Lord commanded: they were made.
God fixed them forever,
gave a law which shall not pass away.

God exalts the strength of the people,
is the praise of all the saints,
of the sons and daughters of Israel,
of the people to whom he comes close.
(Alleluia!)

Glory be to the Father… (Ps 148:1-6, 14)

Psalm Prayer
O glorious God,
your whole creation sings your marvellous work;
may heaven's praise so echo in our hearts
that we may be good stewards of the earth;
through Jesus Christ our Lord. Amen.

Scripture reading
As he who called you is holy, be holy yourselves in all
your conduct; for it is written, 'You shall be holy, for I am
holy.' (1 Peter 1:15-16)

The reading is followed by a pause for silent reflection.

The Sign of the Cross is made at the beginning of the
Gospel Canticle.

Gospel Canticle – The Benedictus
Blessed be the Lord, the God of Israel;
he has come to his people and set them free.
He has raised up for us a mighty saviour,
born of the house of his servant David.

Through his holy prophets he promised of old
that he would save us from our enemies,
from the hands of all who hate us.
He promised to show mercy to our fathers
and to remember his holy covenant.

This was the oath he swore to our father Abraham:
to set us free from the hands of our enemies,
free to worship him without fear,
holy and righteous in his sight all the days of our life.

You, my child, shall be called the prophet of the Most High
for you will go before the Lord to prepare his way,
to give his people knowledge of salvation
by forgiving them their sins.

In the tender compassion of our God
the dawn from on high shall break upon us,
to shine on those who dwell in darkness
and the shadow of death,
and to guide our feet on the road of peace.

Glory be to the Father … (Lk 1:68-79)

Silent thanksgiving is made for the following:
For the gift of life …
For God's merciful love …
For the work of peace-makers …

During the Lord's Prayer the hands may be opened and
extended.

Our Father, who art in heaven,
hallowed be thy name.
Thy kingdom come.
Thy will be done on earth as it is in heaven.
Give us this day our daily bread,
and forgive us our trespasses
as we forgive those who trespass against us,
and lead us not into temptation,
but deliver us from evil.

Concluding Prayer
Lord Jesus, eternal splendour,
on this day which is given us by the Father's love,
do not let us lose sight of you
but always bring us back to the light of your face,
for you live and reign for ever and ever. Amen.

The Sign of the Cross is made as the Blessing is said.

May God the Father and the Son bless us in the unity of the Holy Spirit. Amen.

To the holy and undivided Trinity,
to the Father of all good gifts,
to the humanity of our Lord Jesus Christ, crucified and risen,
be all praise, honour and adoration
at this time and forevermore.

May the souls of the faithful departed through the mercy of God rest in peace. Amen.

Week 1 Monday Evening: Vespers

The Sign of the Cross is made while the opening verse is said.

O God, come to my assistance.
O Lord, make haste to help me.

Glory be to the Father, and to the Son, and to the Holy Spirit: as it was in the beginning, is now, and ever shall be, world without end. Amen. (Alleluia.)

A candle may be lit in front of a Cross, a Bible, an icon or a statue during the thanksgiving for the light.

O joyful light of the holy glory of the Immortal Father, heavenly, holy, blessed Jesus Christ!
Now that we have come to the sun's hour of rest,
the lights of evening round us shine.
We praise the Father, the Son and the Holy Spirit, One God.
Worthy are you, O Lord,
at all times to be praised with undefiled tongue,
O Son of God, O giver of life!
Therefore you are glorified throughout the universe.

Incense may be burned while the following psalm verses are said:

Let my prayer arise before you like incense,
the raising of my hands like an evening sacrifice.

I have called to you, Lord; hasten to help me!
Hear my prayer when I cry to you!

Glory be to the Father ... (Ps 141:2, 1)

Psalm
(Alleluia!)
I love the Lord, for the Lord has heard
the cry of my appeal.
The Lord was attentive to me
in the day when I called.

They surrounded me, the snares of death,
with the anguish of the tomb;
they caught me, sorrow and distress.
I called on the Lord 's name.

O Lord, my God, deliver me!

How gracious is the Lord, and just;
our God has compassion.
The Lord protects the simple hearts;
I was helpless so God saved me.

Turn back, my soul, to your rest
for the Lord has been good,
and has kept my soul from death,
(my eyes from tears,)
my feet from stumbling.

I will walk in the presence of the Lord
in the land of the living.

Glory be to the Father ... (Ps 116:1-9)

Psalm Prayer

As we walk through the valley of the shadow of death,
may we call upon your name,
raise the cup of salvation,
and so proclaim your death, O Lord,
until you come in glory. Amen.

Canticle

The law of the Spirit of life in Christ Jesus
has set us free from the law of sin and of death.
For all who are led by the Spirit of God are children of God:
We have received a spirit of adoption.

When we cry, 'Abba! Father!' it is that very Spirit
bearing witness with our spirit that we are children of God,
and if children, then heirs,
heirs of God and joint heirs with Christ.

The sufferings of this present time
are not worth comparing with the glory
about to be revealed to us.
For the creation waits with eager longing
for the revealing of the children of God.

Glory be to the Father … (Romans 8:2,14,15b-19, alt.)

Psalm of Praise
(Alleluia!)
My soul, give praise to the Lord;
I will praise the Lord all my days,
make music to my God while I live.

It is the Lord who keeps faith for ever,
who is just to those who are oppressed.
It is God who gives bread to the hungry,
the Lord who sets prisoners free,

the Lord who gives sight to the blind,
who raises up those who are bowed down,
the Lord, who protects the stranger
and upholds the widow and orphan.

It is the Lord who loves the just
but thwarts the path of the wicked.
The Lord will reign for ever,
Zion's God, from age to age.
(Alleluia!)

Glory be to the Father ... (Ps 146:1-2, 6b-9)

Psalm Prayer
Lord of all,
our breath and being come from you,
yet our earthly end is dust;
as you loose the bound and feed the hungry,
so bring us in your mercy
through the grave and gate of death
to the feast of eternal life,
where you reign for evermore. Amen.

Scripture reading

In Christ the whole fullness of deity dwells bodily. He is
the head of every ruler and authority. When you were
buried with him in baptism you were also raised with him
through faith in the power of God, who raised him from
the dead. (Col 2:9, 10a, 12)

The reading is followed by a pause for silent reflection.

The Sign of the Cross is made at the beginning of the
Gospel Canticle. Incense may be burned.

Gospel Canticle – The Magnificat

My soul proclaims the greatness of the Lord,
my spirit rejoices in God my Saviour;
for he has looked with favour on his lowly servant,
and from this day all generations will call me blessed.

The Almighty has done great things for me:
holy is his Name.
He has mercy on those who fear him
in every generation.

He has shown the strength of his arm,
he has scattered the proud in their conceit.
He has cast down the mighty from their thrones,
and has lifted up the lowly.
He has filled the hungry with good things,
and has sent the rich away empty.

He has come to the help of his servant Israel
for he has remembered his promise of mercy,

the promise he made to our fathers,
to Abraham and his children for ever.

Glory be to the Father … (Lk 1:46-55)

Silent intercession is made for the following intentions:
For all the nations of the world …
For all who minister in the Church …
For the sick and the aged …

During the Lord's Prayer the hands may be opened and
extended.

Our Father, who art in heaven,
hallowed be thy name.
Thy kingdom come.
Thy will be done on earth as it is in heaven.
Give us this day our daily bread,
and forgive us our trespasses
as we forgive those who trespass against us,
and lead us not into temptation,
but deliver us from evil.

Concluding Prayer

In the peace of the evening,
we come to you, Lord God.
May your word free our hearts
from the cares of this day.
As we experience your forgiveness in Jesus,
may we too forgive in him
our brothers and sisters who have injured us.
We ask this in his name,
Jesus, the Christ, our Lord. Amen.

The Sign of the Cross is made as the Blessing is said.

May God the Father and the Son bless us in the unity of
the Holy Spirit. Amen.

To the holy and undivided Trinity,
to the Father of all good gifts,
to the humanity of our Lord Jesus Christ, crucified and risen,
be all praise, honour and adoration
at this time and forevermore.

May the souls of the faithful departed through the mercy
of God rest in peace. Amen.

Week 1 Tuesday Morning: Lauds

The Sign of the Cross is traced on the lips while the opening verse is said.

O Lord, open my lips.
And my mouth shall praise your name.

Glory be to the Father, and to the Son, and to the Holy Spirit: as it was in the beginning, is now, and ever shall be, world without end. Amen. (Alleluia.)

A candle may be lit in front of a Cross, a Bible, an icon or a statue during the invocation of the light.

Glory be to God who has shown us the light!
Lead me from darkness to light.
Lead me from sadness to joy.
Lead me from death to immortality.
Glory be to God who has shown us the light!

A deep bow or other gesture of reverence may be made while the following psalm verses are said:

Come, ring out our joy to the Lord;
hail the rock who saves us.

O that today you would listen to God's voice!
'Harden not your hearts'.

Glory be to the Father… (Ps 95:1, 7b, 8a)

Psalm

Lord, you are my shepherd;
there is nothing I shall want.
Fresh and green are the pastures
where you give me repose.
Near restful waters you lead me,
to revive my drooping spirit.

You guide me along the right path;
you are true to your name.
If I should walk in the valley of darkness
no evil would I fear.
You are there with your crook and your staff;
with these you give me comfort.

You have prepared a banquet for me
in the sight of my foes.
My head you have anointed with oil;
my cup is overflowing.

Surely goodness and kindness shall follow me
all the days of my life.
In the Lord's own house shall I dwell
for ever and ever.

Glory be to the Father … (Ps 23)

Psalm Prayer

O God, our sovereign and shepherd,
who brought again your Son Jesus Christ
from the valley of death,
comfort us with your protecting presence
and your angels of goodness and love,
that we also may come home
and dwell with him in your house for ever. Amen.

Canticle

Hear the word of the Lord, O nations,
and declare it in the coastlands far away;
say, 'He who scattered Israel will gather him,
and will keep him as a shepherd a flock.'

For the Lord has ransomed Jacob,
and has redeemed him from hands too strong for him.
They shall come and sing aloud on the height of Zion,
and they shall be radiant over the goodness of the Lord,

over the grain, the wine, and the oil,
and over the young of the flock and the herd;
their life shall become like a watered garden,
and they shall never languish again.

Then shall the young women rejoice in the dance,
and the young men and the old shall be merry.
I will turn their mourning into joy,
I will comfort them, and give them gladness for sorrow.

Glory be to the Father … (Jer 31:10-13)

Psalm of Praise

(Alleluia!)
Praise the Lord from the heavens,
praise God in the heights.
Praise God, all you angels,
praise him, all you hosts.

Praise God, sun and moon,
praise him, shining stars.
Praise God, highest heavens
and the waters above the heavens.

Let them praise the name of the Lord.
The Lord commanded: they were made.
God fixed them forever,
gave a law which shall not pass away.

God exalts the strength of the people,
is the praise of all the saints,
of the sons and daughters of Israel,
of the people to whom he comes close.
(Alleluia!)

Glory be to the Father… (Ps 148:1-6, 14)

Psalm Prayer
O glorious God,
your whole creation sings your marvellous work;
may heaven's praise so echo in our hearts
that we may be good stewards of the earth;
through Jesus Christ our Lord. Amen.

Scripture reading

If then there is any encouragement in Christ, any consolation from love, any sharing in the Spirit, any compassion and sympathy, make my joy complete: be of the same mind, having the same love, being in full accord and of one mind. Do nothing from selfish ambition or conceit, but in humility regard others as better than yourselves. (Phil 2:1-3)

The reading is followed by a pause for silent reflection.

The Sign of the Cross is made at the beginning of the Gospel Canticle.

Gospel Canticle – The Benedictus

Blessed be the Lord, the God of Israel;
he has come to his people and set them free.
He has raised up for us a mighty saviour,
born of the house of his servant David.

Through his holy prophets he promised of old
that he would save us from our enemies,
from the hands of all who hate us.
He promised to show mercy to our fathers
and to remember his holy covenant.

This was the oath he swore to our father Abraham:
to set us free from the hands of our enemies,
free to worship him without fear,
holy and righteous in his sight all the days of our life.

You, my child, shall be called the prophet of the Most High
for you will go before the Lord to prepare his way,
to give his people knowledge of salvation
by forgiving them their sins.

In the tender compassion of our God
the dawn from on high shall break upon us,
to shine on those who dwell in darkness
and the shadow of death,
and to guide our feet on the road of peace.

Glory be to the Father … (Lk 1:68-79)

Silent thanksgiving is made for the following:
For God's revelation of himself in his Word …
For the benefits of human labour …
For God's call to each individual person …

During the Lord's Prayer the hands may be opened and
extended.

Our Father, who art in heaven,
hallowed be thy name.
Thy kingdom come.
Thy will be done on earth as it is in heaven.
Give us this day our daily bread,
and forgive us our trespasses
as we forgive those who trespass against us,
and lead us not into temptation,
but deliver us from evil.

Concluding Prayer
Father of Jesus Christ,
open our hearts to your word
and to the power of the Spirit.
Give us love to discover your will
and strength to carry it out today;
for you are light,
for ever and ever. Amen.

The Sign of the Cross is made as the Blessing is said.

May Christ, the only Son of God, bless and help us.
Amen.

To the holy and undivided Trinity,
to the Father of all good gifts,
to the humanity of our Lord Jesus Christ, crucified and risen,
be all praise, honour and adoration
at this time and forevermore.

May the souls of the faithful departed through the mercy
of God rest in peace. Amen.

Week 1 Tuesday Evening: Vespers

The Sign of the Cross is made while the opening verse is said.

O God, come to my assistance.
O Lord, make haste to help me.

Glory be to the Father, and to the Son, and to the Holy Spirit: as it was in the beginning, is now, and ever shall be, world without end. Amen. (Alleluia.)

A candle may be lit in front of a Cross, a Bible, an icon or a statue during the thanksgiving for the light.

O joyful light of the holy glory of the Immortal Father, heavenly, holy, blessed Jesus Christ!
Now that we have come to the sun's hour of rest, the lights of evening round us shine.
We praise the Father, the Son and the Holy Spirit, One God.
Worthy are you, O Lord,
at all times to be praised with undefiled tongue,
O Son of God, O giver of life!
Therefore you are glorified throughout the universe.

Incense may be burned while the following psalm verses are said:

Let my prayer arise before you like incense,
the raising of my hands like an evening sacrifice.

I have called to you, Lord; hasten to help me!
Hear my prayer when I cry to you!

Glory be to the Father... (Ps 141:2, 1)

Psalm
The Lord is my light and my help;
whom shall I fear?
The Lord is the stronghold of my life;
before whom shall I shrink?

When evildoers draw near
to devour my flesh,
it is they, my enemies and foes,
who stumble and fall.

Though an army encamp against me
my heart would not fear.
Though war break out against me
even then would I trust.

There is one thing I ask of the Lord,
for this I long,
to live in the house of the Lord,
all the days of my life,
to savour the sweetness of the Lord,
to behold his temple.

For God makes me safe in his tent
in the day of evil.
God hides me in the shelter of his tent,

on a rock I am secure.
And now my head shall be raised
above my foes who surround me
and I shall offer within God's tent a sacrifice of joy.
I will sing and make music for the Lord.

Glory be to the Father … (Ps 27:1-6)

Psalm Prayer
God, our light and our salvation,
illuminate our lives,
that we may see your goodness in the land of the living,
and, looking on your beauty,
may be changed into the likeness
of Jesus Christ our Lord. Amen.

Canticle
Praise the Lord, all you nations!

Christ was revealed in flesh,
vindicated in spirit.
Praise the Lord, all you nations!

Christ was seen by angels,
proclaimed among Gentiles.
Praise the Lord, all you nations!

Christ was believed in throughout the world,
taken up in glory.
Praise the Lord, all you nations!

Glory be to the Father … (1 Tim 3:16, alt.)

Psalm of Praise

(Alleluia!)
My soul, give praise to the Lord;
I will praise the Lord all my days,
make music to my God while I live.

It is the Lord who keeps faith for ever,
who is just to those who are oppressed.
It is God who gives bread to the hungry,
the Lord who sets prisoners free,

the Lord who gives sight to the blind,
who raises up those who are bowed down,
the Lord, who protects the stranger
and upholds the widow and orphan.

It is the Lord who loves the just
but thwarts the path of the wicked.
The Lord will reign for ever,
Zion's God, from age to age.
(Alleluia!)

Glory be to the Father … (Ps 146:1-2, 6b-9)

Psalm Prayer

Lord of all,
our breath and being come from you,
yet our earthly end is dust;
as you loose the bound and feed the hungry,
so bring us in your mercy
through the grave and gate of death

to the feast of eternal life,
where you reign for evermore. Amen.

Scripture reading
Come to him, a living stone, though rejected by mortals
yet chosen and precious in God's sight, and like living
stones, let yourselves be built into a spiritual house, to be
a holy priesthood, to offer spiritual sacrifices acceptable to
God through Jesus Christ. (1 Peter 2:4-5)

The reading is followed by a pause for silent reflection.

*The Sign of the Cross is made at the beginning of the
Gospel Canticle. Incense may be burned.*

Gospel Canticle – The Magnificat
My soul proclaims the greatness of the Lord,
my spirit rejoices in God my Saviour;
for he has looked with favour on his lowly servant,
and from this day all generations will call me blessed.

The Almighty has done great things for me:
holy is his Name.
He has mercy on those who fear him
in every generation.

He has shown the strength of his arm,
he has scattered the proud in their conceit.
He has cast down the mighty from their thrones,
and has lifted up the lowly.
He has filled the hungry with good things,
and has sent the rich away empty.

He has come to the help of his servant Israel
for he has remembered his promise of mercy,
the promise he made to our fathers,
to Abraham and his children for ever.

Glory be to the Father ... (Lk 1:46-55)

Silent intercession is made for the following intentions:
For the unity of the Church ...
For all who work in public service ...
For the hungry and the destitute ...

During the Lord's Prayer the hands may be opened and
extended.

Our Father, who art in heaven,
hallowed be thy name.
Thy kingdom come.
Thy will be done on earth as it is in heaven.
Give us this day our daily bread,
and forgive us our trespasses
as we forgive those who trespass against us,
and lead us not into temptation,
but deliver us from evil.

Concluding Prayer

Father,
we thank you for showing us your mercy today;
may that mercy extend to all those
whom you entrust to our prayer;
and may it bring your peace to all people,
through Jesus Christ, our Lord. Amen.

The Sign of the Cross is made as the Blessing is said.

May Christ, the only Son of God, bless and help us.
Amen.

To the holy and undivided Trinity,
to the Father of all good gifts,
to the humanity of our Lord Jesus Christ, crucified and risen,
be all praise, honour and adoration
at this time and forevermore.

May the souls of the faithful departed through the mercy
of God rest in peace. Amen.

Week 1 Wednesday Morning: Lauds

The Sign of the Cross is traced on the lips while the opening verse is said.

O Lord, open my lips.
And my mouth shall praise your name.

Glory be to the Father, and to the Son, and to the Holy Spirit: as it was in the beginning, is now, and ever shall be, world without end. Amen. (Alleluia.)

A candle may be lit in front of a Cross, a Bible, an icon or a statue during the invocation of the light.

Glory be to God who has shown us the light!
Lead me from darkness to light.
Lead me from sadness to joy.
Lead me from death to immortality.
Glory be to God who has shown us the light!

A deep bow or other gesture of reverence may be made while the following psalm verses are said:

Come, ring out our joy to the Lord;
hail the rock who saves us.

O that today you would listen to God's voice!
'Harden not your hearts'.

Glory be to the Father... (Ps 95:1, 7b, 8a)

Psalm

To you, O Lord, I lift up my soul.
My God, I trust you, let me not be disappointed;
do not let my enemies triumph.
Those who hope in you shall not be disappointed,
but only those who wantonly break faith.

Lord, make me know your ways.
Lord , teach me your paths.
Make me walk in your truth, and teach me,
for you are God my saviour.

In you I hope all the day long
because of your goodness, O Lord.
Remember your mercy, Lord,
and the love you have shown from of old.
Do not remember the sins of my youth.
In your love remember me.

The Lord is good and upright,
showing the path to those who stray,
guiding the humble in the right path,
and teaching the way to the poor.

Glory be to the Father … (Ps 25:1-9)

Psalm Prayer
Free us, God of mercy,
from all that keeps us from you;
relieve the misery of the anxious and the ashamed
and fill us with the hope of peace;
through Jesus Christ our Lord. Amen.
Canticle

Surely God is my salvation;
I will trust, and will not be afraid,
for the Lord God is my strength and my might;
he has become my salvation.

With joy you will draw water from the wells of salvation.
Give thanks to the Lord, call on his name;
make known his deeds among the nations;
proclaim that his name is exalted.

Sing praises to the Lord, for he has done gloriously;
let this be known in all the earth.
Shout aloud and sing for joy, O royal Zion,
for great in your midst is the Holy One of Israel.

Glory be to the Father … (Is 12:2-6)

Psalm of Praise
(Alleluia!)
Praise the Lord from the heavens,
praise God in the heights.
Praise God, all you angels,
praise him, all you hosts.

Praise God, sun and moon,
praise him, shining stars.
Praise God, highest heavens
and the waters above the heavens.

Let them praise the name of the Lord.
The Lord commanded: they were made.
God fixed them forever,

gave a law which shall not pass away.

God exalts the strength of the people,
is the praise of all the saints,
of the sons and daughters of Israel,
of the people to whom he comes close.
(Alleluia!)

Glory be to the Father... (Ps 148:1-6, 14)

Psalm Prayer
O glorious God,
your whole creation sings your marvellous work;
may heaven's praise so echo in our hearts
that we may be good stewards of the earth;
through Jesus Christ our Lord. Amen.

Scripture reading

As God's chosen ones, holy and beloved, clothe yourselves with compassion, kindness, humility, meekness,
and patience. Bear with one another and, if anyone has a
complaint against another, forgive each other; just as the
Lord has forgiven you, so you also must forgive.
(Col 3:12-13)

The reading is followed by a pause for silent reflection.

The Sign of the Cross is made at the beginning of the
Gospel Canticle.

Gospel Canticle – The Benedictus
Blessed be the Lord, the God of Israel;
he has come to his people and set them free.
He has raised up for us a mighty saviour,
born of the house of his servant David.

Through his holy prophets he promised of old
that he would save us from our enemies,
from the hands of all who hate us.
He promised to show mercy to our fathers
and to remember his holy covenant.

This was the oath he swore to our father Abraham:
to set us free from the hands of our enemies,
free to worship him without fear,
holy and righteous in his sight all the days of our life.

You, my child, shall be called the prophet of the Most High
for you will go before the Lord to prepare his way,
to give his people knowledge of salvation
by forgiving them their sins.

In the tender compassion of our God
the dawn from on high shall break upon us,
to shine on those who dwell in darkness
and the shadow of death,
and to guide our feet on the road of peace.

Glory be to the Father … (Lk 1:68-79)

Silent thanksgiving is made for the following:
For all human deeds of kindness and compassion …
For the action of the Holy Spirit in the world …
For the grace and power of the sacraments …

During the Lord's Prayer the hands may be opened and
extended.

Our Father, who art in heaven,
hallowed be thy name.
Thy kingdom come.
Thy will be done on earth as it is in heaven.
Give us this day our daily bread,
and forgive us our trespasses
as we forgive those who trespass against us,
and lead us not into temptation,
but deliver us from evil.

Concluding Prayer
Father almighty,
you revealed to us that you are light.
Help us to live our lives in your radiance
and so be in fellowship with one another.
We ask this through Jesus Christ, our Lord. Amen.

The Sign of the Cross is made as the Blessing is said.

May God light the fire of his love in our hearts. Amen.

To the holy and undivided Trinity,
to the Father of all good gifts,
to the humanity of our Lord Jesus Christ, crucified and risen,
be all praise, honour and adoration
at this time and forevermore.

May the souls of the faithful departed through the mercy
of God rest in peace. Amen.

Week 1 Wednesday Evening: Vespers

O God, come to my assistance.
O Lord, make haste to help me.

Glory be to the Father, and to the Son, and to the Holy Spirit: as it was in the beginning, is now, and ever shall be, world without end. Amen. (Alleluia.)

O joyful light of the holy glory of the Immortal Father,
heavenly, holy, blessed Jesus Christ!
Now that we have come to the sun's hour of rest,
the lights of evening round us shine.
We praise the Father, the Son and the Holy Spirit, One God.
Worthy are you, O Lord,
at all times to be praised with undefiled tongue,
O Son of God, O giver of life!
Therefore you are glorified throughout the universe.

Let my prayer arise before you like incense,
the raising of my hands like an evening sacrifice.

I have called to you, Lord; hasten to help me!
Hear my prayer when I cry to you!

Glory be to the Father ... (Ps 141:2, 1)

Psalm
Out of the depths I cry to you, O Lord,
Lord, hear my voice!
O let your ears be attentive
to the voice of my pleading.

If you, O Lord, should mark our guilt,
Lord, who would survive?
But with you is found forgiveness:
for this we revere you.

My soul is waiting for the Lord.
I count on God's word.
My soul is longing for the Lord
more than those who watch for daybreak.
(Let the watchers count on daybreak
and Israel on the Lord.)

Because with the Lord there is mercy
and fullness of redemption,
Israel indeed God will redeem
from all its iniquity.

Glory be to the Father ... (Ps 130)

Psalm Prayer

Father, we commend to your faithful love
those who are crying from the depths;
help them to watch and pray
through their time of darkness,
in sure hope of the dawn of your
forgiveness and redemption;
through Jesus Christ our Lord. Amen.

Canticle

Great and amazing are your deeds,
Lord God the Almighty!
Just and true are your ways,
King of the nations!

Lord, who will not fear and glorify your name?
For you alone are holy.
All nations will come and worship before you,
for your judgements have been revealed.

Glory be to the Father … (Rev 15:3-4)

Psalm of Praise

(Alleluia!)
My soul, give praise to the Lord;
I will praise the Lord all my days,
make music to my God while I live.

It is the Lord who keeps faith for ever,
who is just to those who are oppressed.
It is God who gives bread to the hungry,
the Lord who sets prisoners free,

the Lord who gives sight to the blind,
who raises up those who are bowed down,
the Lord, who protects the stranger
and upholds the widow and orphan.

It is the Lord who loves the just
but thwarts the path of the wicked.
The Lord will reign for ever,
Zion's God, from age to age.
(Alleluia!)

Glory be to the Father ... (Ps 146:1-2, 6b-9)

Psalm Prayer
Lord of all,
our breath and being come from you,
yet our earthly end is dust;
as you loose the bound and feed the hungry,
so bring us in your mercy
through the grave and gate of death
to the feast of eternal life,
where you reign for evermore. Amen.

Scripture reading
If we have died with Christ, we believe that we will also
live with him. We know that Christ, being raised from the
dead, will never die again; death no longer has dominion
over him. The death he died, he died to sin, once for all;
but the life he lives, he lives to God. So you also must
consider yourselves dead to sin and alive to God in Christ
Jesus. (Rom 6:8-11)

The reading is followed by a pause for silent reflection.

The Sign of the Cross is made at the beginning of the Gospel Canticle. Incense may be burned.

Gospel Canticle – The Magnificat
My soul proclaims the greatness of the Lord,
my spirit rejoices in God my Saviour;
for he has looked with favour on his lowly servant,
and from this day all generations will call me blessed.

The Almighty has done great things for me:
holy is his Name.
He has mercy on those who fear him
in every generation.

He has shown the strength of his arm,
he has scattered the proud in their conceit.
He has cast down the mighty from their thrones,
and has lifted up the lowly.
He has filled the hungry with good things,
and has sent the rich away empty.

He has come to the help of his servant Israel
for he has remembered his promise of mercy,
the promise he made to our fathers,
to Abraham and his children for ever.

Glory be to the Father ... (Lk 1:46-55)

Silent intercession is made for the following intentions:
For those who struggle to believe …
For those who work in agriculture and food production …
For those who mourn…

During the Lord's Prayer the hands may be opened and
extended.

Our Father, who art in heaven,
hallowed be thy name.
Thy kingdom come.
Thy will be done on earth as it is in heaven.
Give us this day our daily bread,
and forgive us our trespasses
as we forgive those who trespass against us,
and lead us not into temptation,
but deliver us from evil.

Concluding Prayer
It is for you that we live, Lord our God,
and to you we have consecrated this day;
perfect and purify our offering,
so that our prayer of thanksgiving may rise to you,
in Jesus, your Son, our Lord. Amen.

The Sign of the Cross is made as the Blessing is said.

May God light the fire of his love in our hearts. Amen.

To the holy and undivided Trinity,
to the Father of all good gifts,
to the humanity of our Lord Jesus Christ, crucified and risen,
be all praise, honour and adoration
at this time and forevermore.

May the souls of the faithful departed through the mercy
of God rest in peace. Amen.

Week 1 Thursday Morning: Lauds

The Sign of the Cross is traced on the lips while the opening verse is said.

O Lord, open my lips.
And my mouth shall praise your name.

Glory be to the Father, and to the Son, and to the Holy Spirit: as it was in the beginning, is now, and ever shall be, world without end. Amen. (Alleluia.)

A candle may be lit in front of a Cross, a Bible, an icon or a statue during the invocation of the light.

Glory be to God who has shown us the light!
Lead me from darkness to light.
Lead me from sadness to joy.
Lead me from death to immortality.
Glory be to God who has shown us the light!

A deep bow or other gesture of reverence may be made while the following psalm verses are said:

Come, ring out our joy to the Lord;
hail the rock who saves us.

O that today you would listen to God's voice!
'Harden not your hearts'.

Glory be to the Father… (Ps 95:1, 7b, 8a)

Psalm

Ring out your joy to the Lord, O you just;
for praise is fitting for loyal hearts.

Give thanks to the Lord upon the harp,
with a ten-stringed lute play your songs.
Sing to the Lord a song that is new,
play loudly, with all your skill.

For the word of the Lord is faithful
and all his works done in truth.
The Lord loves justice and right
and fills the earth with love.

By God's word the heavens were made,
by the breath of his mouth all the stars.
God collects the waves of the ocean;
and stores up the depths of the sea.

Let all the earth fear the Lord,
all who live in the world stand in awe.
For God spoke, it came to be.
God commanded; it sprang into being.

The Lord foils the designs of the nations,
and defeats the plans of the peoples.
The counsel of the Lord stands forever,
the plans of God's heart from age to age.

Glory be to the Father …(Ps 33:1-11)

Psalm Prayer

Feed your people, Lord,
with your holy word
and free us from the emptiness of our wrongful desires,
that we may sing the new song of salvation
through Jesus Christ our Lord. Amen.

Canticle

O God of my ancestors and Lord of mercy,
who have made all things by your word,
give me the wisdom that sits by your throne,
and do not reject me from among your servants.

With you is wisdom, she who knows your works
and was present when you made the world;
she understands what is pleasing in your sight
and what is right according to your commandments.

Send her forth from the holy heavens,
and from the throne of your glory send her,
that she may labour at my side,
and that I may learn what is pleasing to you.

For she knows and understands all things,
and she will guide me wisely in my actions
and guard me with her glory.

Glory be to the Father … (Wis 9:1, 4, 9-11)

Psalm of Praise

(Alleluia!)
Praise the Lord from the heavens,
praise God in the heights.
Praise God, all you angels,
praise him, all you hosts.

Praise God, sun and moon,
praise him, shining stars.
Praise God, highest heavens
and the waters above the heavens.

Let them praise the name of the Lord.
The Lord commanded: they were made.
God fixed them forever,
gave a law which shall not pass away.

God exalts the strength of the people,
is the praise of all the saints,
of the sons and daughters of Israel,
of the people to whom he comes close.
(Alleluia!)

Glory be to the Father... (Ps 148:1-6, 14)

Psalm Prayer
O glorious God,
your whole creation sings your marvellous work;
may heaven's praise so echo in our hearts
that we may be good stewards of the earth;
through Jesus Christ our Lord. Amen.

Scripture reading

You, beloved, are not in darkness, for that day to surprise
you like a thief; for you are all children of light and children
of the day; we are not of the night or of darkness.
(1 Thess 5:4-5)

The reading is followed by a pause for silent reflection.

*The Sign of the Cross is made at the beginning of the
Gospel Canticle.*

Gospel Canticle – The Benedictus

Blessed be the Lord, the God of Israel;
he has come to his people and set them free.
He has raised up for us a mighty saviour,
born of the house of his servant David.

Through his holy prophets he promised of old
that he would save us from our enemies,
from the hands of all who hate us.
He promised to show mercy to our fathers
and to remember his holy covenant.

This was the oath he swore to our father Abraham:
to set us free from the hands of our enemies,
free to worship him without fear,
holy and righteous in his sight all the days of our life.

You, my child, shall be called the prophet of the Most High
for you will go before the Lord to prepare his way,
to give his people knowledge of salvation
by forgiving them their sins.

In the tender compassion of our God
the dawn from on high shall break upon us,
to shine on those who dwell in darkness
and the shadow of death,
and to guide our feet on the road of peace.

Glory be to the Father ... (Lk 1:68-79)

Silent thanksgiving is made for the following:
For the example of holy lives ...
For signs of the coming of the Reign of God ...
For the communion of saints ...

During the Lord's Prayer the hands may be opened and
extended.

Our Father, who art in heaven,
hallowed be thy name.
Thy kingdom come.
Thy will be done on earth as it is in heaven.
Give us this day our daily bread,
and forgive us our trespasses
as we forgive those who trespass against us,
and lead us not into temptation,
but deliver us from evil.

Concluding Prayer

God, our Father,
when you gave us your Son,
your light came into the world.
May we welcome him in our lives,
and thus be a light for our brothers and sisters.
We ask this through Jesus Christ, our Lord. Amen.

The Sign of the Cross is made as the Blessing is said.

May God be merciful to us and bless us. Amen.

To the holy and undivided Trinity,
to the Father of all good gifts,
to the humanity of our Lord Jesus Christ, crucified and risen,
be all praise, honour and adoration
at this time and forevermore.

May the souls of the faithful departed through the mercy
of God rest in peace. Amen.

Week 1 Thursday Evening: Vespers

The Sign of the Cross is made while the opening verse is said.

O God, come to my assistance.
O Lord, make haste to help me.

Glory be to the Father, and to the Son, and to the Holy Spirit: as it was in the beginning, is now, and ever shall be, world without end. Amen. (Alleluia.)

A candle may be lit in front of a Cross, a Bible, an icon or a statue during the thanksgiving for the light.

O joyful light of the holy glory of the Immortal Father,
heavenly, holy, blessed Jesus Christ!
Now that we have come to the sun's hour of rest,
the lights of evening round us shine.
We praise the Father, the Son and the Holy Spirit, One God.
Worthy are you, O Lord,
at all times to be praised with undefiled tongue,
O Son of God, O giver of life!
Therefore you are glorified throughout the universe.

Incense may be burned while the following psalm verses are said:

Let my prayer arise before you like incense,
the raising of my hands like an evening sacrifice.

I have called to you, Lord; hasten to help me!
Hear my prayer when I cry to you!

Glory be to the Father ... (Ps 141:2, 1)

Psalm
O Lord, you search me and you know me,
you know my resting and my rising,
you discern my purpose from afar.
You mark when I walk or lie down,
all my ways lie open to you.

Before ever a word is on my tongue
you know it, O Lord, through and through.
Behind and before you besiege me,
your hand ever laid upon me.
Too wonderful for me, this knowledge,
too high, beyond my reach.

O where can I go from your spirit,
Or where can I flee from your face?
If I climb the heavens, you are there.
If I lie in the grave, you are there.

If I take the wings of the dawn
and dwell at the sea's furthest end,
even there your hand would lead me,
your right hand would hold me fast.

If I say: 'Let the darkness hide me
and the light around me be night,'

even darkness is not dark for you
and the night is as clear as the day.
For it was you who created my being,
knit me together in my mother's womb.

Glory be to the Father …(Ps 139:1-13)

Psalm Prayer
Creator God,
may every breath we take be for your glory,
may every footstep show you as our way,
that, trusting in your presence in this world,
we may, beyond this life, still be with you
where you are alive and reign
for ever and ever. Amen.

Canticle
Give thanks to the Father,
who has enabled you to share
in the inheritance of the saints in the light.

He has rescued us from the power of darkness
and transferred us into the kingdom of his beloved Son,
in whom we have redemption,
the forgiveness of sins.

He is the image of the invisible God,
the firstborn of all creation;
for in him all things in heaven and on earth were created,
things visible and invisible.

All things have been created
through him and for him.
He himself is before all things,
and in him all things hold together.

He is the head of the body, the church;
he is the beginning,
the firstborn from the dead,
so that he might come to have first place in everything.

For in him all the fullness of God was pleased to dwell,
and through him God was pleased
to reconcile to himself all things,
whether on earth or in heaven,
by making peace through the blood of his cross.

Glory be to the Father … (Col 1:12-20)

Psalm of Praise
(Alleluia!)
My soul, give praise to the Lord;
I will praise the Lord all my days,
make music to my God while I live.

It is the Lord who keeps faith for ever,
who is just to those who are oppressed.
It is God who gives bread to the hungry,
the Lord who sets prisoners free,

the Lord who gives sight to the blind,
who raises up those who are bowed down,
the Lord, who protects the stranger
and upholds the widow and orphan.

It is the Lord who loves the just
but thwarts the path of the wicked.
The Lord will reign for ever,
Zion's God, from age to age.
(Alleluia!)

Glory be to the Father … (Ps 146:1-2, 6b-9)

Psalm Prayer
Lord of all,
our breath and being come from you,
yet our earthly end is dust;
as you loose the bound and feed the hungry,
so bring us in your mercy
through the grave and gate of death
to the feast of eternal life,
where you reign for evermore. Amen.

Scripture reading
In the one Spirit we were all baptised into one body —
Jews or Greeks, slaves or free — and we were all made to
drink of one Spirit. (1 Cor 12:13)

The reading is followed by a pause for silent reflection.

The Sign of the Cross is made at the beginning of the
Gospel Canticle. Incense may be burned.

Gospel Canticle – The Magnificat
My soul proclaims the greatness of the Lord,
my spirit rejoices in God my Saviour;
for he has looked with favour on his lowly servant,
and from this day all generations will call me blessed.

The Almighty has done great things for me:
holy is his Name.
He has mercy on those who fear him
in every generation.

He has shown the strength of his arm,
he has scattered the proud in their conceit.
He has cast down the mighty from their thrones,
and has lifted up the lowly.
He has filled the hungry with good things,
and has sent the rich away empty.

He has come to the help of his servant Israel
for he has remembered his promise of mercy,
the promise he made to our fathers,
to Abraham and his children for ever.

Glory be to the Father ... (Lk 1:46-55)

Silent intercession is made for the following intentions:
For all preachers and evangelists …
For those who work to support families and communities …
For refugees and all displaced people …

During the Lord's Prayer the hands may be opened and extended.

Our Father, who art in heaven,
hallowed be thy name.
Thy kingdom come.
Thy will be done on earth as it is in heaven.
Give us this day our daily bread,
and forgive us our trespasses
as we forgive those who trespass against us,
and lead us not into temptation,
but deliver us from evil.

Concluding Prayer
Lord God, ever faithful,
see us gathered before you
as the day draws to a close;
confirm our hearts in your love,
and keep alive in us
the memory of your goodness and kindness,
which have appeared in Jesus Christ, our Lord. Amen.

The Sign of the Cross is made as the Blessing is said.

May God be merciful to us and bless us. Amen.

To the holy and undivided Trinity,
to the Father of all good gifts,
to the humanity of our Lord Jesus Christ, crucified and risen,
be all praise, honour and adoration
at this time and forevermore.

May the souls of the faithful departed through the mercy
of God rest in peace. Amen.

Week 1 Friday Morning: Lauds

The Sign of the Cross is traced on the lips while the opening verse is said.

O Lord, open my lips.
And my mouth shall praise your name.

Glory be to the Father, and to the Son, and to the Holy Spirit: as it was in the beginning, is now, and ever shall be, world without end. Amen. (Alleluia.)

A candle may be lit in front of a Cross, a Bible, an icon or a statue during the invocation of the light.

Glory be to God who has shown us the light!
Lead me from darkness to light.
Lead me from sadness to joy.
Lead me from death to immortality.
Glory be to God who has shown us the light!

A deep bow or other gesture of reverence may be made while the following psalm verses are said:

Come, ring out our joy to the Lord;
hail the rock who saves us.

O that today you would listen to God's voice!
'Harden not your hearts'.

Glory be to the Father… (Ps 95:1, 7b, 8a)

Psalm

Have mercy on me, God, in your kindness.
In your compassion blot out my offence.
O wash me more and more from my guilt
and cleanse me from my sin.

My offences truly I know them;
my sin is always before me.
Against you, you alone, have I sinned;
what is evil in your sight I have done.

That you may be justified when you give sentence
and be without reproach when you judge,
O see, in guilt I was born,
a sinner was I conceived.

Indeed you love truth in the heart;
then in the secret of my heart teach me wisdom.
O purify me, then I shall be clean;
O wash me, I shall be whiter than snow.

Make me hear rejoicing and gladness
that the bones you have crushed may revive.
From my sins turn away your face
and blot out all my guilt

Glory be to the Father ... (Ps 51:1-10)

Psalm Prayer

Take away, good Lord, the sin that corrupts us;
give us the sorrow that heals and the joy that praises
and restore by grace your own image within us,
that we may take our place among your people;
in Jesus Christ our Lord. Amen.

Canticle

Hear, you who are far away, what I have done;
and you who are near, acknowledge my might.
The sinners in Zion are afraid;
trembling has seized the godless:

'Who among us can live with the devouring fire?
Who among us can live with everlasting flames?'
Those who walk righteously and speak uprightly,
who despise the gain of oppression,

who wave away a bribe instead of accepting it,
who stop their ears from hearing of bloodshed
and shut their eyes from looking on evil,

they will live on the heights;
their refuge will be the fortresses of rocks;
their food will be supplied, their water assured.

Glory be to the Father … (Is 33:13-16)

Psalm of Praise

(Alleluia!)
Praise the Lord from the heavens,
praise God in the heights.
Praise God, all you angels,
praise him, all you hosts.

Praise God, sun and moon,
praise him, shining stars.
Praise God, highest heavens
and the waters above the heavens.

Let them praise the name of the Lord.
The Lord commanded: they were made.
God fixed them forever,
gave a law which shall not pass away.

God exalts the strength of the people,
is the praise of all the saints,
of the sons and daughters of Israel,
of the people to whom he comes close.
(Alleluia!)

Glory be to the Father... (Ps 148:1-6, 14)

Psalm Prayer

O glorious God,
your whole creation sings your marvellous work;
may heaven's praise so echo in our hearts
that we may be good stewards of the earth;
through Jesus Christ our Lord. Amen.

Scripture reading

In the days of his flesh, Jesus offered up prayers and
supplications, with loud cries and tears, to the one who
was able to save him from death, and he was heard
because of his reverent submission. Although he was a
Son, he learned obedience through what he suffered; and
having been made perfect, he became the source of eternal
salvation for all who obey him, having been designated by
God a high priest according to the order of Melchizedek.
(Hebrews 5:7-10)

The reading is followed by a pause for silent reflection.

The Sign of the Cross is made at the beginning of the
Gospel Canticle.

Gospel Canticle – The Benedictus
Blessed be the Lord, the God of Israel;
he has come to his people and set them free.
He has raised up for us a mighty saviour,
born of the house of his servant David.

Through his holy prophets he promised of old
that he would save us from our enemies,
from the hands of all who hate us.
He promised to show mercy to our fathers
and to remember his holy covenant.

This was the oath he swore to our father Abraham:
to set us free from the hands of our enemies,
free to worship him without fear,
holy and righteous in his sight all the days of our life.

You, my child, shall be called the prophet of the Most High
for you will go before the Lord to prepare his way,
to give his people knowledge of salvation
by forgiving them their sins.

In the tender compassion of our God
the dawn from on high shall break upon us,
to shine on those who dwell in darkness
and the shadow of death,
and to guide our feet on the road of peace.

Glory be to the Father ... (Lk 1:68-79)

Silent thanksgiving is made for the following:
For Christ's humble example on the cross ...
For the assurance of the forgiveness of sin ...
For the example of all who lay down their lives for
others ...

During the Lord's Prayer the hands may be opened and
extended.

Our Father, who art in heaven,
hallowed be thy name.
Thy kingdom come.
Thy will be done on earth as it is in heaven.
Give us this day our daily bread,
and forgive us our trespasses
as we forgive those who trespass against us,
and lead us not into temptation,
but deliver us from evil.

Concluding Prayer

Lord Jesus,
your food was to do the will of your Father.
Make us attentive this day to the call of the Spirit,
and give us the strength to respond in humility,
for you are our help, for ever and ever. Amen.

The Sign of the Cross is made as the Blessing is said.

May the King of Friday lead us into paradise. Amen.

To the holy and undivided Trinity,
to the Father of all good gifts,
to the humanity of our Lord Jesus Christ, crucified and risen,
be all praise, honour and adoration
at this time and forevermore.

May the souls of the faithful departed through the mercy
of God rest in peace. Amen.

Week 1 Friday Evening: Vespers

The Sign of the Cross is made while the opening verse is said.

O God, come to my assistance.
O Lord, make haste to help me.

Glory be to the Father, and to the Son, and to the Holy Spirit: as it was in the beginning, is now, and ever shall be, world without end. Amen. (Alleluia.)

A candle may be lit in front of a Cross, a Bible, an icon or a statue during the thanksgiving for the light.

O joyful light of the holy glory of the Immortal Father,
heavenly, holy, blessed Jesus Christ!
Now that we have come to the sun's hour of rest,
the lights of evening round us shine.
We praise the Father, the Son and the Holy Spirit, One God.
Worthy are you, O Lord,
at all times to be praised with undefiled tongue,
O Son of God, O giver of life!
Therefore you are glorified throughout the universe.

Incense may be burned while the following psalm verses are said:

Let my prayer arise before you like incense,
the raising of my hands like an evening sacrifice.
I have called to you, Lord; hasten to help me!
Hear my prayer when I cry to you!

Glory be to the Father… (Ps 141:2, 1)

Psalm

I will praise you, Lord, you have rescued me
and have not let my enemies rejoice over me.

O Lord, I cried to you for help
and you, my God, have healed me.
O Lord, you have raised my soul from the dead,
restored me to life from those who sink into the grave.

Sing psalms to the Lord, you faithful ones,
give thanks to his holy name.
God's anger lasts a moment; God's favour all through life.
At night there are tears, but joy comes with dawn.

I said to myself in my good fortune:
'Nothing will ever disturb me.'
Your favour had set me on a mountain fastness,
then you hid your face and I was put to confusion.

To you, Lord, I cried,
to my God I made appeal:
'What profit would my death be, my going to the grave?
Can dust give you praise or proclaim your truth?'

The Lord listened and had pity.
The Lord came to my help.
For me you have changed my mourning into dancing,
you removed my sackcloth and clothed me with joy.
So my soul sings psalms to you unceasingly.
O Lord my God, I will thank you for ever.

Glory be to the Father … (Ps 30)

Psalm Prayer

Lord, you hide your face
when we trust in ourselves;
strip us of false security
and re-clothe us in your praise,
that we may know you
as the one who raises us from death,
as you raised your Son, our Saviour Jesus Christ. Amen.

Canticle

Though he was in the form of God,
Jesus did not regard equality with God
as something to be exploited,
but emptied himself, taking the form of a slave,
being born in human likeness.

And being found in human form,
he humbled himself
and became obedient to the point of death –
even death on a cross.

Therefore God also highly exalted him
and gave him the name that is above every name,
so that at the name of Jesus every knee should bend,
in heaven and on earth and under the earth,
and every tongue should confess that Jesus Christ is Lord,
to the glory of God the Father.

Glory be to the Father … (Phil 2:6-11)

Psalm of Praise

(Alleluia!)

My soul, give praise to the Lord;
I will praise the Lord all my days,
make music to my God while I live.

It is the Lord who keeps faith for ever,
who is just to those who are oppressed.
It is God who gives bread to the hungry,
the Lord who sets prisoners free,

the Lord who gives sight to the blind,
who raises up those who are bowed down,
the Lord, who protects the stranger
and upholds the widow and orphan.

It is the Lord who loves the just
but thwarts the path of the wicked.
The Lord will reign for ever,
Zion's God, from age to age.
(Alleluia!)

Glory be to the Father ... (Ps 146:1-2, 6b-9)

Psalm Prayer

Lord of all,
our breath and being come from you,
yet our earthly end is dust;
as you loose the bound and feed the hungry,
so bring us in your mercy
through the grave and gate of death
to the feast of eternal life,
where you reign for evermore. Amen.

Scripture reading

If anyone does sin, we have an advocate with the Father,
Jesus Christ the righteous; and he is the atoning sacrifice
for our sins, and not for ours only but also for the sins of
the whole world. Now by this we may be sure that we
know him, if we obey his commandments. Whoever says,
'I have come to know him', but does not obey his
commandments, is a liar, and in such a person the truth
does not exist. (1 John 2:1-4)

The reading is followed by a pause for silent reflection.

The Sign of the Cross is made at the beginning of the
Gospel Canticle. Incense may be burned.

Gospel Canticle – The Magnificat

My soul proclaims the greatness of the Lord,
my spirit rejoices in God my Saviour;
for he has looked with favour on his lowly servant,
and from this day all generations will call me blessed.

The Almighty has done great things for me:
holy is his Name.
He has mercy on those who fear him
in every generation.

He has shown the strength of his arm,
he has scattered the proud in their conceit.
He has cast down the mighty from their thrones,
and has lifted up the lowly.
He has filled the hungry with good things,
and has sent the rich away empty.

He has come to the help of his servant Israel
for he has remembered his promise of mercy,
the promise he made to our fathers,
to Abraham and his children for ever.

Glory be to the Father … (Lk 1:46-55)

Silent intercession is made for the following intentions:
For all who suffer because of their faith in Christ …
For all who are unjustly deprived of their liberty …
For the faithful departed …

During the Lord's Prayer the hands may be opened and
extended.

Our Father, who art in heaven,
hallowed be thy name.
Thy kingdom come.
Thy will be done on earth as it is in heaven.
Give us this day our daily bread,
and forgive us our trespasses
as we forgive those who trespass against us,
and lead us not into temptation,
but deliver us from evil.

Concluding Prayer
May the memory of your death on the cross, Lord Jesus,
confirm our hearts in faith and hope;
then we shall live together in your love,
waiting for your coming,
for you are our Saviour, for ever and ever. Amen.

The Sign of the Cross is made as the Blessing is said.
May the King of Friday lead us into paradise. Amen.

To the holy and undivided Trinity,
to the Father of all good gifts,
to the humanity of our Lord Jesus Christ, crucified and risen,
be all praise, honour and adoration
at this time and forevermore.

May the souls of the faithful departed through the mercy
of God rest in peace. Amen.

Week 1 Saturday Morning: Lauds

The Sign of the Cross is traced on the lips while the opening verse is said.

O Lord, open my lips.
And my mouth shall praise your name.

Glory be to the Father, and to the Son, and to the Holy Spirit: as it was in the beginning, is now, and ever shall be, world without end. Amen. (Alleluia.)

A candle may be lit in front of a Cross, a Bible, an icon or a statue during the invocation of the light.

Glory be to God who has shown us the light!
Lead me from darkness to light.
Lead me from sadness to joy.
Lead me from death to immortality.
Glory be to God who has shown us the light!

A deep bow or other gesture of reverence may be made while the following psalm verses are said:

Come, ring out our joy to the Lord;
hail the rock who saves us.

O that today you would listen to God's voice!
'Harden not your hearts'.

Glory be to the Father... (Ps 95:1, 7b, 8a)

Psalm

The Lord is king, with majesty enrobed;
the Lord is robed with might,
and girded round with power.

The world you made firm, not to be moved;
your throne has stood firm from of old.
From all eternity, O Lord, you are.

The waters have lifted up, O Lord,
the waters have lifted up their voice,
the waters have lifted up their thunder.

Greater than the roar of mighty waters,
more glorious than the surgings of the sea,
the Lord is glorious on high.

Truly your decrees are to be trusted.
Holiness is fitting to your house,
O Lord, until the end of time.

Glory be to the Father ... (Ps 93)

Psalm Prayer

Christ our King,
you put on the apparel of our nature
and raised us to your glory;
reign from your royal throne
above the chaos of this world,
that all may see the victory you have won
and trust in your salvation;
for your glory's sake. Amen.

Canticle

I will sing to the Lord, for he has triumphed gloriously;
horse and rider he has thrown into the sea.
The Lord is my strength and my might,
and he has become my salvation;

this is my God, and I will praise him,
my father's God, and I will exalt him.
Your right hand, O Lord, glorious in power –
your right hand, O Lord, shattered the enemy.

In your steadfast love
you led the people whom you redeemed;
you guided them by your strength to your holy abode.
You brought them in and planted them
on the mountain of your own possession,
the place, O Lord, that you made your abode,
the sanctuary, O Lord, that your hands have established.

Glory be to the Father ...(Ex 15:1b-2, 6, 13, 17)

Psalm of Praise

(Alleluia!)
Praise the Lord from the heavens,
praise God in the heights.
Praise God, all you angels,
praise him, all you hosts.

Praise God, sun and moon,
praise him, shining stars.
Praise God, highest heavens
and the waters above the heavens.

Let them praise the name of the Lord.
The Lord commanded: they were made.
God fixed them forever,
gave a law which shall not pass away.

God exalts the strength of the people,
is the praise of all the saints,
of the sons and daughters of Israel,
of the people to whom he comes close.
(Alleluia!)

Glory be to the Father... (Ps 148:1-6, 14)

Psalm Prayer
O glorious God,
your whole creation sings your marvellous work;
may heaven's praise so echo in our hearts
that we may be good stewards of the earth;
through Jesus Christ our Lord. Amen.

Scripture reading
When the fullness of time had come, God sent his Son,
born of a woman, born under the law, in order to redeem
those who were under the law, so that we might receive
adoption as children. (Gal 4:4-5)

The reading is followed by a pause for silent reflection.

The Sign of the Cross is made at the beginning of the Gospel Canticle.

Gospel Canticle – The Benedictus

Blessed be the Lord, the God of Israel;
he has come to his people and set them free.
He has raised up for us a mighty saviour,
born of the house of his servant David.

Through his holy prophets he promised of old
that he would save us from our enemies,
from the hands of all who hate us.
He promised to show mercy to our fathers
and to remember his holy covenant.

This was the oath he swore to our father Abraham:
to set us free from the hands of our enemies,
free to worship him without fear,
holy and righteous in his sight all the days of our life.

You, my child, shall be called the prophet of the Most High
for you will go before the Lord to prepare his way,
to give his people knowledge of salvation
by forgiving them their sins.

In the tender compassion of our God
the dawn from on high shall break upon us,
to shine on those who dwell in darkness
and the shadow of death,
and to guide our feet on the road of peace.

Glory be to the Father ... (Lk 1:68-79)

Silent thanksgiving is made for the following:
For the presence of Christ with us …
For Mary's example of fidelity …
For the gift of friendship …

During the Lord's Prayer the hands may be opened and extended.

Our Father, who art in heaven,
hallowed be thy name.
Thy kingdom come.
Thy will be done on earth as it is in heaven.
Give us this day our daily bread,
and forgive us our trespasses
as we forgive those who trespass against us,
and lead us not into temptation,
but deliver us from evil.

Concluding Prayer
God our Father,
you chose Mary from the lowly among your people,
and her one desire was to be your handmaid.
Through her intercession,
grant us poverty of spirit,
and reveal to us the mysteries of your kingdom,
through Jesus, the Christ, our Lord. Amen.

The Sign of the Cross is made as the Blessing is said.

May the most holy Mother of God intercede for us with
the Lord. Amen.

To the holy and undivided Trinity,
to the Father of all good gifts,
to the humanity of our Lord Jesus Christ, crucified and risen,
be all praise, honour and adoration
at this time and forevermore.

May the souls of the faithful departed through the mercy
of God rest in peace. Amen.

Week 1 Saturday Evening: Vespers

The Sign of the Cross is made while the opening verse is said.

O God, come to my assistance.
O Lord, make haste to help me.

Glory be to the Father, and to the Son, and to the Holy Spirit: as it was in the beginning, is now, and ever shall be, world without end. Amen. (Alleluia.)

A candle may be lit in front of a Cross, a Bible, an icon or a statue during the thanksgiving for the light.

O joyful light of the holy glory of the Immortal Father,
heavenly, holy, blessed Jesus Christ!
Now that we have come to the sun's hour of rest,
the lights of evening round us shine.
We praise the Father, the Son and the Holy Spirit, One God.
Worthy are you, O Lord,
at all times to be praised with undefiled tongue,
O Son of God, O giver of life!
Therefore you are glorified throughout the universe.

Incense may be burned while the following psalm verses are said:

Let my prayer arise before you like incense,
the raising of my hands like an evening sacrifice.

I have called to you, Lord; hasten to help me!
Hear my prayer when I cry to you!

Glory be to the Father... (Ps 141:2, 1)

Psalm
(Alleluia!)
I will thank the Lord with all my heart
in the meeting of the just and their assembly.
Great are the works of the Lord,
To be pondered by all who love them.

Majestic and glorious God's work,
whose justice stands firm for ever.
God makes us remember these wonders.
The Lord is compassion and love.

God gives food to those who fear him;
keeps his covenant ever in mind;
shows mighty works to his people
by giving them the land of the nations.

God's works are justice and truth,
God's precepts are all of them sure,
standing firm for ever and ever;
they are made in uprightness and truth.

God has sent deliverance to his people
and established his covenant for ever.
Holy is God's name, to be feared.

To fear the Lord is the first stage of wisdom;
all who do so prove themselves wise.
God's praise shall last for ever.

Glory be to the Father ... (Ps 111)

Psalm Prayer
Gracious God, you are full of compassion;
may we who long for your kingdom to come
rejoice to do your will
and acknowledge your power alone to save;
through Jesus Christ our Lord. Amen.

Canticle
You are worthy, our Lord and God,
to receive glory and honour and power,
for you created all things,
and by your will they existed and were created.

You are worthy to take the scroll
and to open its seals,
for you were slaughtered and by your blood
you ransomed for God
saints from every tribe and language and people and nation.

You have made them to be a kingdom
and priests serving our God,
and they will reign on earth.

Worthy is the Lamb that was slaughtered
to receive power and wealth

and wisdom and might
and honour and glory and blessing!

Glory be to the Father ... (Rev 4:11, 5:9, 10, 12)

Psalm of Praise
(Alleluia!)
My soul, give praise to the Lord;
I will praise the Lord all my days,
make music to my God while I live.

It is the Lord who keeps faith for ever,
who is just to those who are oppressed.
It is God who gives bread to the hungry,
the Lord who sets prisoners free,

the Lord who gives sight to the blind,
who raises up those who are bowed down,
the Lord, who protects the stranger
and upholds the widow and orphan.

It is the Lord who loves the just
but thwarts the path of the wicked.
The Lord will reign for ever,
Zion's God, from age to age.
(Alleluia!)

Glory be to the Father ... (Ps 146:1-2, 6b-9)

Psalm Prayer
Lord of all,
our breath and being come from you,

yet our earthly end is dust;
as you loose the bound and feed the hungry,
so bring us in your mercy
through the grave and gate of death
to the feast of eternal life,
where you reign for evermore. Amen.

Scripture reading

He saved us, not because of any works of righteousness
that we had done, but according to his mercy, through the
water of rebirth and renewal by the Holy Spirit. This
Spirit he poured out on us richly through Jesus Christ our
Saviour, so that, having been justified by his grace, we
might become heirs according to the hope of eternal life.
(Titus 3:5-7)

The reading is followed by a pause for silent reflection.

The Sign of the Cross is made at the beginning of the
Gospel Canticle. Incense may be burned.

Gospel Canticle – The Magnificat

My soul proclaims the greatness of the Lord,
my spirit rejoices in God my Saviour;
for he has looked with favour on his lowly servant,
and from this day all generations will call me blessed.

The Almighty has done great things for me:
holy is his Name.
He has mercy on those who fear him
in every generation.

He has shown the strength of his arm,
he has scattered the proud in their conceit.
He has cast down the mighty from their thrones,
and has lifted up the lowly.
He has filled the hungry with good things,
and has sent the rich away empty.

He has come to the help of his servant Israel
for he has remembered his promise of mercy,
the promise he made to our fathers,
to Abraham and his children for ever.

Glory be to the Father … (Lk 1:46-55)

Silent intercession is made for the following intentions:
For the building-up of the Church …
For the outpouring of the Holy Spirit on the world …
For the coming of the Kingdom …

During the Lord's Prayer the hands may be opened and
extended.

Our Father, who art in heaven,
hallowed be thy name.
Thy kingdom come.
Thy will be done on earth as it is in heaven.
Give us this day our daily bread,
and forgive us our trespasses
as we forgive those who trespass against us,
and lead us not into temptation,
but deliver us from evil.

Concluding Prayer

God our Father,
when Jesus was dying for us
Mary his mother stood by his side
in the darkness which covered the earth.
In the unending dawn of the resurrection,
may she stand as a sign of our sure hope,
that we will one day be with you,
that Light that will shine for ever and ever. Amen.

The Sign of the Cross is made as the Blessing is said.

Through the prayers of your most pure mother and of all
your saints, Lord Jesus Christ, have mercy on us and save
us. Amen.

To the holy and undivided Trinity,
to the Father of all good gifts,
to the humanity of our Lord Jesus Christ, crucified and risen,
be all praise, honour and adoration
at this time and forevermore.

May the souls of the faithful departed through the mercy
of God rest in peace. Amen.

Week 2 Sunday Morning: Lauds

The Sign of the Cross is traced on the lips while the opening verse is said.

O Lord, open my lips.
And my mouth shall praise your name.

Glory be to the Father, and to the Son, and to the Holy Spirit: as it was in the beginning, is now, and ever shall be, world without end. Amen. (Alleluia.)

A candle may be lit in front of a Cross, a Bible, an icon or a statue during the invocation of the light.
Now that I have risen from sleep,
I thank you, Lord of creation,
for keeping me safe throughout the night!
I bless you for the morning light and cry to you in adoration:
Holy, Holy, Holy are you, O Lord!
Have mercy on me and on the whole world!

A deep bow or other gesture of reverence may be made while the following psalm verses are said:

Come, ring out our joy to the Lord;
hail the rock who saves us.

O that today you would listen to God's voice!
'Harden not your hearts'.

Glory be to the Father… (Ps 95:1, 7b, 8a)

Psalm

O God, you are my God, for you I long;
for you my soul is thirsting.
My body pines for you
like a dry, weary land without water.
So I gaze on you in the sanctuary
to see your strength and your glory.

For your love is better than life,
my lips will speak your praise.
So I will bless you all my life,
in your name I will lift up my hands.
My soul shall be filled as with a banquet,
my mouth shall praise you with joy.

On my bed I remember you.
On you I muse through the night
for you have been my help;
in the shadow of your wings I rejoice.
My soul clings to you;
your right hand holds me fast.

Glory be to the Father ... (Ps 63:1-9)

Psalm Prayer
To you we come, radiant Lord,
the goal of all our desiring,
beyond all earthly beauty;
gentle protector, strong deliverer,
in the night you are our confidence;
from first light be our joy;
through Jesus Christ our Lord. Amen.

Canticle

Blessed are you, O Lord, God of our ancestors,
and to be praised and highly exalted for ever;

And blessed is your glorious, holy name,
and to be highly praised and highly exalted for ever.

Blessed are you in the temple of your holy glory,
and to be extolled and highly glorified for ever.

Blessed are you who look into the depths from your
throne on the cherubim,
and to be praised and highly exalted for ever.

Blessed are you on the throne of your kingdom,
and to be extolled and highly exalted for ever.

Blessed are you in the firmament of heaven,
and to be sung and glorified for ever.

Glory be to the Father... (Dan 3:52-57)

Psalm of Praise

(Alleluia!)
Praise God in his holy place,
Sing praise in the mighty heavens.
Sing praise for God's powerful deeds,
Praise God's surpassing greatness.

Sing praise with sound of trumpet,
Sing praise with lute and harp.
Sing praise with timbrel and dance,
Sing praise with strings and pipes.

Sing praise with resounding cymbals,
Sing praise with clashing of cymbals.
Let everything that lives and that breathes
give praise to the Lord.
(Alleluia!)

Glory be to the Father … (Ps 150)

Psalm Prayer
God of life and love,
whose Son was victorious over sin and death,
make us alive with his life,
that the whole world may resound with your praise;
through Jesus Christ our Lord. Amen.

Scripture reading
This is the one who came by water and blood, Jesus
Christ, not with the water only but with the water and
the blood. And the Spirit is the one that testifies, for the
Spirit is the truth. There are three that testify:the Spirit
and the water and the blood, and these three agree. If we
receive human testimony, the testimony of God is greater;
for this is the testimony of God that he has testified to his
Son. Those who believe in the Son of God have the
testimony in their hearts. Those who do not believe in
God have made him a liar by not believing in the testimony
that God has given concerning his Son. (1 John 5:6-10)

The reading is followed by a pause for silent reflection.

The Sign of the Cross is made at the beginning of the Gospel Canticle.

Gospel Canticle – The Benedictus
Blessed be the Lord, the God of Israel;
he has come to his people and set them free.
He has raised up for us a mighty saviour,
born of the house of his servant David.

Through his holy prophets he promised of old
that he would save us from our enemies,
from the hands of all who hate us.
He promised to show mercy to our fathers
and to remember his holy covenant.

This was the oath he swore to our father Abraham:
to set us free from the hands of our enemies,
free to worship him without fear,
holy and righteous in his sight all the days of our life.

You, my child, shall be called the prophet of the Most High
for you will go before the Lord to prepare his way,
to give his people knowledge of salvation
by forgiving them their sins.

In the tender compassion of our God
the dawn from on high shall break upon us,
to shine on those who dwell in darkness
and the shadow of death,
and to guide our feet on the road of peace.

Glory be to the Father … (Lk 1:68-79)

Silent thanksgiving is made for the following:

For the promise of eternity in Christ's resurrection from the dead …

For the new life received in baptism …

For the fruitfulness of creation …

During the Lord's Prayer the hands may be opened and extended.

Our Father, who art in heaven,
hallowed be thy name.
Thy kingdom come.
Thy will be done on earth as it is in heaven.
Give us this day our daily bread,
and forgive us our trespasses
as we forgive those who trespass against us,
and lead us not into temptation,
but deliver us from evil.

Concluding Prayer

Father of mercy,
your love embraces everyone
and through the resurrection of your Son
you call us into your wonderful light.
Dispel our darkness
and make us a people with one heart and one voice,
forever singing your praise,
in Jesus, the Christ, our Lord. Amen.

The Sign of the Cross is made as the Blessing is said.

May Christ our Lord, by the power of his resurrection
have mercy on us and save us. Amen.

To the holy and undivided Trinity,
to the Father of all good gifts,
to the humanity of our Lord Jesus Christ, crucified and risen,
be all praise, honour and adoration
at this time and forevermore.

May the souls of the faithful departed through the mercy
of God rest in peace. Amen.

Week 2 Sunday Evening: Vespers

The Sign of the Cross is made while the opening verse is said.

O God, come to my assistance.
O Lord, make haste to help me.

Glory be to the Father, and to the Son, and to the Holy Spirit: as it was in the beginning, is now, and ever shall be, world without end. Amen. (Alleluia.)

A candle may be lit in front of a Cross, a Bible, an icon or a statue during the thanksgiving for the light.

Now that the day has come to a close,
I thank you, Lord of creation,
for keeping me safe throughout this day!
I bless you for the evening light and cry to you in adoration:
Holy, Holy, Holy are you, O Lord!
Have mercy on me and on the whole world!

Incense may be burned while the following psalm verses are said:

Let my prayer arise before you like incense,
the raising of my hands like an evening sacrifice.

I have called to you, Lord; hasten to help me!
Hear my prayer when I cry to you!

Glory be to the Father... (Ps 141:2, 1)

Psalm

(Alleluia!)

O give thanks to the Lord who is good,
whose love endures for ever.
Give thanks to the God of gods,
whose love endures for ever.
Give thanks to the Lord of lords,
whose love endures for ever;

who alone has wrought marvellous works,
whose love endures for ever;
whose wisdom it was made the skies,
whose love endures for ever;
who fixed the earth firmly on the seas,
whose love endures for ever.

It was God who made the great lights,
whose love endures for ever;
the sun to rule in the day,
whose love endures for ever;
the moon and the stars in the night,
whose love endures for ever.

The first-born of the Egyptians God smote,
whose love endures for ever;
and brought Israel out from the midst,
whose love endures for ever;
arm outstretched, with powerful hand,
whose love endures for ever.

Glory be to the Father ... (Ps 136:1-12)

Psalm Prayer

Remember us, O God, and shape our history,
form our inward eyes
to see the shadow of the life-giving cross
in the turbulence of our time;
for his sake who died for all, Christ our Lord. Amen.

Canticle

(Alleluia!)
Salvation and glory and power to our God!

Praise our God, all you his servants,
and all who fear him, small and great.

For the Lord our God, the Almighty, reigns.
Let us rejoice and exult and give him the glory.

For the marriage of the Lamb has come,
and his bride has made herself ready.

Blessed are those who are invited
to the marriage supper of the Lamb.

Glory be to the Father … (Rev 19:1b, 5b, 6b, 7, 9b)

Psalm of Praise

(Alleluia!)
O praise the Lord, Jerusalem!
Zion, praise your God!

God has strengthened the bars of your gates,
and has blessed the children within you;
has established peace on your borders,
and feeds you with finest wheat.

God sends out word to the earth
and swiftly runs the command.
God showers down snow white as wool,
and scatters hoarfrost like ashes.

God makes his word known to Jacob,
to Israel his laws and decrees.
God has not dealt thus with others nations;
has not taught them divine decrees.
(Alleluia!)

Glory be to the Father ... (Ps 147:12-16, 19-20)

Psalm Prayer
Compassionate God,
as you know each star you have created,
so you know the secrets of every heart;
in your loving mercy bring to your table
all who are fearful and broken,
all who are wounded and needy,
that our hungers may be satisfied in the city of your peace;
through Christ who is our peace. Amen.

Scripture reading

Christ has been raised from the dead, the first fruits of those who have died. For since death came through a human being, the resurrection of the dead has also come through a human being; for as all die in Adam, so all will be made alive in Christ. (1 Cor 15:20-22)

The reading is followed by a pause for silent reflection.

The Sign of the Cross is made at the beginning of the Gospel Canticle. Incense may be burned.

Gospel Canticle – The Magnificat

My soul proclaims the greatness of the Lord,
my spirit rejoices in God my Saviour;
for he has looked with favour on his lowly servant,
and from this day all generations will call me blessed.

The Almighty has done great things for me:
holy is his Name.
He has mercy on those who fear him
in every generation.

He has shown the strength of his arm,
he has scattered the proud in their conceit.
He has cast down the mighty from their thrones,
and has lifted up the lowly.
He has filled the hungry with good things,
and has sent the rich away empty.

He has come to the help of his servant Israel
for he has remembered his promise of mercy,
the promise he made to our fathers,
to Abraham and his children for ever.

Glory be to the Father … (Lk 1:46-55)

Silent intercession is made for the following intentions:
For the mission and ministry of the Church …
For friends, relations and neighbours …
For all in any kind of need …

During the Lord's Prayer the hands may be opened and
extended.

Our Father, who art in heaven,
hallowed be thy name.
Thy kingdom come.
Thy will be done on earth as it is in heaven.
Give us this day our daily bread,
and forgive us our trespasses
as we forgive those who trespass against us,
and lead us not into temptation,
but deliver us from evil.

Concluding Prayer

We give you thanks, Lord our God,
for this day, now drawing to a close.
May our prayer, rising before you like incense,
be pleasing to you;
and may our outstretched hands be filled with your mercy,
through Jesus, your Son, our Lord. Amen.

The Sign of the Cross is made as the Blessing is said.

May Christ our Lord, by the power of his resurrection
have mercy on us and save us. Amen.

To the holy and undivided Trinity,
to the Father of all good gifts,
to the humanity of our Lord Jesus Christ, crucified and risen,
be all praise, honour and adoration
at this time and forevermore.

May the souls of the faithful departed through the mercy
of God rest in peace. Amen.

Week 2 Monday Morning: Lauds

O Lord, open my lips.
And my mouth shall praise your name.

Glory be to the Father, and to the Son, and to the Holy Spirit: as it was in the beginning, is now, and ever shall be, world without end. Amen. (Alleluia.)

A candle may be lit in front of a Cross, a Bible, an icon or a statue during the invocation of the light.
Now that I have risen from sleep,
I thank you, Lord of creation,
for keeping me safe throughout the night!
I bless you for the morning light and cry to you in adoration:
Holy, Holy, Holy are you, O Lord!
Have mercy on me and on the whole world!

A deep bow or other gesture of reverence may be made while the following psalm verses are said:

Come, ring out our joy to the Lord;
hail the rock who saves us.

O that today you would listen to God's voice!
'Harden not your hearts'.

Glory be to the Father... (Ps 95:1, 7b, 8a)

Psalm

Like the deer that yearns
for running streams,
so my soul is yearning
for you, my God.

My soul is thirsting for God,
the God of my life;
when can I enter and see
the face of God?

My tears have become my bread,
by night, by day,
as I hear it said all the day long:
'Where is your God?'

These things will I remember
as I pour out my soul:
how I would lead the rejoicing crowd
into the house of God,
amid cries of gladness and thanksgiving,
the throng wild with joy.

Why are you cast down, my soul,
why groan within me?
Hope in God; I will praise yet again,
my saviour and my God.

Glory be to the Father ... (Ps 42:1-6)

Psalm Prayer

Come, creator Spirit, source of life;
sustain us when our hearts are heavy
and our wells have run dry,
for you are the Father's gift,
with him who is our living water,
Jesus Christ our Lord. Amen.

Canticle

Blessed are you, O Lord, the God of our ancestor Israel,
for ever and ever.
Yours, O Lord, are the greatness, the power, the glory,
the victory, and the majesty;
for all that is in the heavens and on the earth is yours;
yours is the kingdom, O Lord,
and you are exalted as head above all.

Riches and honour come from you,
and you rule over all.
In your hand are power and might;
and it is in your hand to make great
and to give strength to all.

And now, our God, we give thanks to you
and praise your glorious name.
For all things come from you,
and of your own have we given you.

Glory be to the Father ... (1 Chron 29:10b-13, 14b)

Psalm of Praise

(Alleluia!)
Praise God in his holy place,
Sing praise in the mighty heavens.
Sing praise for God's powerful deeds,
Praise God's surpassing greatness.

Sing praise with sound of trumpet,
Sing praise with lute and harp.
Sing praise with timbrel and dance,
Sing praise with strings and pipes.

Sing praise with resounding cymbals,
Sing praise with clashing of cymbals.
Let everything that lives and that breathes
give praise to the Lord.
(Alleluia!)

Glory be to the Father ... (Ps 150)

Psalm Prayer

God of life and love,
whose Son was victorious over sin and death,
make us alive with his life,
that the whole world may resound with your praise;
through Jesus Christ our Lord. Amen.

Scripture reading

Blessed is anyone who endures temptation. Such a one
has stood the test and will receive the crown of life that the
Lord has promised to those who love him. (James 1:12)

The reading is followed by a pause for silent reflection.

The Sign of the Cross is made at the beginning of the Gospel Canticle.

Gospel Canticle – The Benedictus

Blessed be the Lord, the God of Israel;
he has come to his people and set them free.
He has raised up for us a mighty saviour,
born of the house of his servant David.

Through his holy prophets he promised of old
that he would save us from our enemies,
from the hands of all who hate us.
He promised to show mercy to our fathers
and to remember his holy covenant.

This was the oath he swore to our father Abraham:
to set us free from the hands of our enemies,
free to worship him without fear,
holy and righteous in his sight all the days of our life.

You, my child, shall be called the prophet of the Most High
for you will go before the Lord to prepare his way,
to give his people knowledge of salvation
by forgiving them their sins.

In the tender compassion of our God
the dawn from on high shall break upon us,
to shine on those who dwell in darkness
and the shadow of death,
and to guide our feet on the road of peace.

Glory be to the Father … (Lk 1:68-79)

Silent thanksgiving is made for the following:
For the gift of life …
For God's merciful love …
For the work of peace-makers …

During the Lord's Prayer the hands may be opened and
extended.

Our Father, who art in heaven,
hallowed be thy name.
Thy kingdom come.
Thy will be done on earth as it is in heaven.
Give us this day our daily bread,
and forgive us our trespasses
as we forgive those who trespass against us,
and lead us not into temptation,
but deliver us from evil.

Concluding Prayer
Lord Jesus, eternal splendour,
on this day which is given us by the Father's love,
do not let us lose sight of you
but always bring us back to the light of your face,
for you live and reign for ever and ever. Amen.

The Sign of the Cross is made as the Blessing is said.

May God the Father and the Son bless us in the unity of
the Holy Spirit. Amen.

To the holy and undivided Trinity,
to the Father of all good gifts,
to the humanity of our Lord Jesus Christ, crucified and risen,
be all praise, honour and adoration
at this time and forevermore.

May the souls of the faithful departed through the mercy
of God rest in peace. Amen.

Week 2 Monday Evening: Vespers

The Sign of the Cross is made while the opening verse is said.

O God, come to my assistance.
O Lord, make haste to help me.

Glory be to the Father, and to the Son, and to the Holy Spirit: as it was in the beginning, is now, and ever shall be, world without end. Amen. (Alleluia.)

A candle may be lit in front of a Cross, a Bible, an icon or a statue during the thanksgiving for the light.

Now that the day has come to a close,
I thank you, Lord of creation,
for keeping me safe throughout this day!
I bless you for the evening light and cry to you in adoration:
Holy, Holy, Holy are you, O Lord!
Have mercy on me and on the whole world!

Incense may be burned while the following psalm verses are said:

Let my prayer arise before you like incense,
the raising of my hands like an evening sacrifice.

I have called to you, Lord; hasten to help me!
Hear my prayer when I cry to you!

Glory be to the Father… (Ps 141:2, 1)

Psalm

I trusted, even when I said:
'I am sorely afflicted,'
and when I said in my alarm:
'There is no one I can trust.'

How can I repay the Lord
for his goodness to me?
The cup of salvation I will raise;
I will call on the Lord's name.

My vows to the Lord I will fulfil
before all the people.
O precious in the eyes of the Lord
is the death of the faithful.

Your servant, Lord, your servant am I;
you have loosened my bonds.
A thanksgiving sacrifice I make;
I will call on the Lord's name.

My vows to the Lord I will fulfil
before all the people,
in the courts of the house of the Lord,
in your midst, O Jerusalem.

Glory be to the Father ... (Ps 116:10-19)

Psalm Prayer
As we walk through the valley of the shadow of death,
may we call upon your name,
raise the cup of salvation,
and so proclaim your death, O Lord,
until you come in glory. Amen.

Canticle
The law of the Spirit of life in Christ Jesus
has set us free from the law of sin and of death.
For all who are led by the Spirit of God are children of God:
We have received a spirit of adoption.

When we cry, 'Abba! Father!' it is that very Spirit
bearing witness with our spirit that we are children of God,
and if children, then heirs,
heirs of God and joint heirs with Christ.

The sufferings of this present time
are not worth comparing with the glory
about to be revealed to us.
For the creation waits with eager longing
for the revealing of the children of God.

Glory be to the Father … (Romans 8:2,14,15b-19, alt.)

Psalm of Praise
(Alleluia!)
O praise the Lord, Jerusalem!
Zion, praise your God!

God has strengthened the bars of your gates,
and has blessed the children within you;
has established peace on your borders,
and feeds you with finest wheat.

God sends out word to the earth
and swiftly runs the command.
God showers down snow white as wool,
and scatters hoarfrost like ashes.

God makes his word known to Jacob,
to Israel his laws and decrees.
God has not dealt thus with others nations;
has not taught them divine decrees.
(Alleluia!)

Glory be to the Father … (Ps 147:12-16, 19-20)

Psalm Prayer
Compassionate God,
as you know each star you have created,
so you know the secrets of every heart;
in your loving mercy bring to your table
all who are fearful and broken,
all who are wounded and needy,
that our hungers may be satisfied in the city of your peace;
through Christ who is our peace. Amen.

Scripture reading

You are a chosen race, a royal priesthood, a holy nation, God's own people, in order that you may proclaim the mighty acts of him who called you out of darkness into his marvellous light. Once you were not a people, but now you are God's people; once you had not received mercy, but now you have received mercy. (1 Pet 2:9-10)

The reading is followed by a pause for silent reflection.

The Sign of the Cross is made at the beginning of the Gospel Canticle. Incense may be burned.

Gospel Canticle – The Magnificat

My soul proclaims the greatness of the Lord,
my spirit rejoices in God my Saviour;
for he has looked with favour on his lowly servant,
and from this day all generations will call me blessed.

The Almighty has done great things for me:
holy is his Name.
He has mercy on those who fear him
in every generation.

He has shown the strength of his arm,
he has scattered the proud in their conceit.
He has cast down the mighty from their thrones,
and has lifted up the lowly.
He has filled the hungry with good things,
and has sent the rich away empty.

He has come to the help of his servant Israel
for he has remembered his promise of mercy,
the promise he made to our fathers,
to Abraham and his children for ever.

Glory be to the Father ... (Lk 1:46-55)

Silent intercession is made for the following intentions:
For all the nations of the world ...
For all who minister in the Church ...
For the sick and the aged ...

During the Lord's Prayer the hands may be opened and
extended.

Our Father, who art in heaven,
hallowed be thy name.
Thy kingdom come.
Thy will be done on earth as it is in heaven.
Give us this day our daily bread,
and forgive us our trespasses
as we forgive those who trespass against us,
and lead us not into temptation,
but deliver us from evil.

Concluding Prayer

In the peace of the evening,
we come to you, Lord God.
May your word free our hearts
from the cares of this day.
As we experience your forgiveness in Jesus,
may we too forgive in him
our brothers and sisters who have injured us.
We ask this in his name,
Jesus, the Christ, our Lord. Amen.

The Sign of the Cross is made as the Blessing is said.

May God the Father and the Son bless us in the unity of
the Holy Spirit. Amen.

To the holy and undivided Trinity,
to the Father of all good gifts,
to the humanity of our Lord Jesus Christ, crucified and risen,
be all praise, honour and adoration
at this time and forevermore.

May the souls of the faithful departed through the mercy
of God rest in peace. Amen.

Week 2 Tuesday Morning: Lauds

The Sign of the Cross is traced on the lips while the opening
verse is said.

O Lord, open my lips.
And my mouth shall praise your name.

Glory be to the Father, and to the Son, and to the Holy
Spirit: as it was in the beginning, is now, and ever shall be,
world without end. Amen. (Alleluia.)

A candle may be lit in front of a Cross, a Bible, an icon or
a statue during the invocation of the light.

Now that I have risen from sleep,
I thank you, Lord of creation,
for keeping me safe throughout the night!
I bless you for the morning light and cry to you in adoration:
Holy, Holy, Holy are you, O Lord!
Have mercy on me and on the whole world!

A deep bow or other gesture of reverence may be made
while the following psalm verses are said:

Come, ring out our joy to the Lord;
hail the rock who saves us.

O that today you would listen to God's voice!
'Harden not your hearts'.

Glory be to the Father... (Ps 95:1, 7b, 8a)

Psalm

To my words give ear, O Lord,
give heed to my groaning.
Attend to the sound of my cries,
my King and my God.

It is you whom I invoke, O Lord.
In the morning you hear me;
in the morning I offer you my prayer,
watching and waiting.

You are no God who loves evil;
no sinner is your guest.
The boastful shall not stand their ground
before your face.

But I through the greatness of your love
have access to your house.
I bow down before your holy temple,
filled with awe.

Lead me, Lord, in your justice,
because of those who lie in wait;
make clear your way before me.

All those you protect shall be glad
and ring out their joy.
You shelter them; in you they rejoice,
those who love your name.

Lord, it is you who bless the upright:
you surround them with favour as with a shield.

Glory be to the Father … (Ps 5:1-5a, 7-9, 12-13)

Psalm Prayer

Lord, protect us from the deceit
of flattering tongues and lying lips;
give us words of life which speak your truth
and bless your name;
through Jesus Christ our Lord. Amen.

Canticle

Hear the word of the Lord, O nations,
and declare it in the coastlands far away;
say, 'He who scattered Israel will gather him,
and will keep him as a shepherd a flock.'

For the Lord has ransomed Jacob,
and has redeemed him from hands too strong for him.
They shall come and sing aloud on the height of Zion,
and they shall be radiant over the goodness of the Lord,

over the grain, the wine, and the oil,
and over the young of the flock and the herd;
their life shall become like a watered garden,
and they shall never languish again.
Then shall the young women rejoice in the dance,
and the young men and the old shall be merry.
I will turn their mourning into joy,
I will comfort them, and give them gladness for sorrow.

Glory be to the Father ... (Jer 31:10-13)

Psalm of Praise

(Alleluia!)

Praise God in his holy place,
Sing praise in the mighty heavens.
Sing praise for God's powerful deeds,
Praise God's surpassing greatness.

Sing praise with sound of trumpet,
Sing praise with lute and harp.
Sing praise with timbrel and dance,
Sing praise with strings and pipes.

Sing praise with resounding cymbals,
Sing praise with clashing of cymbals.
Let everything that lives and that breathes
give praise to the Lord.
(Alleluia!)

Glory be to the Father ... (Ps 150)

Psalm Prayer
God of life and love,
whose Son was victorious over sin and death,
make us alive with his life,
that the whole world may resound with your praise;
through Jesus Christ our Lord. Amen.

Scripture reading

The love of Christ urges us on, because we are convinced that one has died for all; therefore all have died. And he died for all, so that those who live might live no longer for themselves, but for him who died and was raised for them. From now on, therefore, we regard no one from a human point of view; even though we once knew Christ from a human point of view, we know him no longer in that way. (2 Cor 5:14-16)

The reading is followed by a pause for silent reflection.

The Sign of the Cross is made at the beginning of the Gospel Canticle.

Gospel Canticle – The Benedictus
Blessed be the Lord, the God of Israel;
he has come to his people and set them free.
He has raised up for us a mighty saviour,
born of the house of his servant David.

Through his holy prophets he promised of old
that he would save us from our enemies,
from the hands of all who hate us.
He promised to show mercy to our fathers
and to remember his holy covenant.

This was the oath he swore to our father Abraham:
to set us free from the hands of our enemies,
free to worship him without fear,
holy and righteous in his sight all the days of our life.

You, my child, shall be called the prophet of the Most High
for you will go before the Lord to prepare his way,
to give his people knowledge of salvation
by forgiving them their sins.

In the tender compassion of our God
the dawn from on high shall break upon us,
to shine on those who dwell in darkness
and the shadow of death,
and to guide our feet on the road of peace.

Glory be to the Father … (Lk 1:68-79)

Silent thanksgiving is made for the following:
For God's revelation of himself in his Word …
For the benefits of human labour …
For God's call to each individual person …

During the Lord's Prayer the hands may be opened and
extended.

Our Father, who art in heaven,
hallowed be thy name.
Thy kingdom come.
Thy will be done on earth as it is in heaven.
Give us this day our daily bread,
and forgive us our trespasses
as we forgive those who trespass against us,
and lead us not into temptation,
but deliver us from evil.

Concluding Prayer

Father of Jesus Christ,
open our hearts to your word
and to the power of the Spirit.
Give us love to discover your will
and strength to carry it out today;
for you are light,
for ever and ever. Amen.

The Sign of the Cross is made as the Blessing is said.

May Christ, the only Son of God, bless and help us.
Amen.

To the holy and undivided Trinity,
to the Father of all good gifts,
to the humanity of our Lord Jesus Christ, crucified and risen,
be all praise, honour and adoration
at this time and forevermore.

May the souls of the faithful departed through the mercy
of God rest in peace. Amen.

Week 2 Tuesday Evening: Vespers

The Sign of the Cross is made while the opening verse is said.

O God, come to my assistance.
O Lord, make haste to help me.

Glory be to the Father, and to the Son, and to the Holy Spirit: as it was in the beginning, is now, and ever shall be, world without end. Amen. (Alleluia.)

A candle may be lit in front of a Cross, a Bible, an icon or a statue during the thanksgiving for the light.

Now that the day has come to a close,
I thank you, Lord of creation,
for keeping me safe throughout this day!
I bless you for the evening light and cry to you in adoration:
Holy, Holy, Holy are you, O Lord!
Have mercy on me and on the whole world!

Incense may be burned while the following psalm verses are said:

Let my prayer arise before you like incense,
the raising of my hands like an evening sacrifice.

I have called to you, Lord; hasten to help me!
Hear my prayer when I cry to you!

Glory be to the Father… (Ps 141:2, 1)

Psalm

O Lord, hear my voice when I call;
have mercy and answer.
Of you my heart has spoken:
'Seek God's face.'

It is your face, O Lord, that I seek;
hide not your face.
Dismiss not your servant in anger;
you have been my help.

Do not abandon or forsake me,
O God my help!
Though father and mother forsake me,
the Lord will receive me.

Instruct me, Lord, in your way;
on an even path lead me.
When they lie in ambush protect me
from my enemies' greed.
False witnesses rise against me,
breathing out fury.

I am sure I shall see the Lord's goodness
in the land of the living.
In the Lord, hold firm and take heart.
Hope in the Lord!

Glory be to the Father … (Ps 27:7-14)

Psalm Prayer

God, our light and our salvation,
illuminate our lives,
that we may see your goodness in the land of the living,
and, looking on your beauty,
may be changed into the likeness of
Jesus Christ our Lord. Amen.

Canticle

Praise the Lord, all you nations!

Christ was revealed in flesh,
vindicated in spirit.
Praise the Lord, all you nations!

Christ was seen by angels,
proclaimed among Gentiles.
Praise the Lord, all you nations!

Christ was believed in throughout the world,
taken up in glory.
Praise the Lord, all you nations!

Glory be to the Father … (1 Tim 3:16, alt.)

Psalm of Praise

(Alleluia!)
O praise the Lord, Jerusalem!
Zion, praise your God!

God has strengthened the bars of your gates,
and has blessed the children within you;
has established peace on your borders,
and feeds you with finest wheat.

God sends out word to the earth
and swiftly runs the command.
God showers down snow white as wool,
and scatters hoarfrost like ashes.

God makes his word known to Jacob,
to Israel his laws and decrees.
God has not dealt thus with others nations;
has not taught them divine decrees.
(Alleluia!)

Glory be to the Father ... (Ps 147:12-16, 19-20)

Psalm Prayer
Compassionate God,
as you know each star you have created,
so you know the secrets of every heart;
in your loving mercy bring to your table
all who are fearful and broken,
all who are wounded and needy,
that our hungers may be satisfied in the city of your peace;
through Christ who is our peace. Amen.

Scripture reading

I appeal to you therefore, brothers and sisters, by the
mercies of God, to present your bodies as a living sacrifice,
holy and acceptable to God, which is your spiritual worship.
Do not be conformed to this world, but be transformed
by the renewing of your minds, so that you may discern
what is the will of God – what is good and acceptable
and perfect. (Rom 12:1-2)

The reading is followed by a pause for silent reflection.

The Sign of the Cross is made at the beginning of the
Gospel Canticle. Incense may be burned.

Gospel Canticle – The Magnificat

My soul proclaims the greatness of the Lord,
my spirit rejoices in God my Saviour;
for he has looked with favour on his lowly servant,
and from this day all generations will call me blessed.

The Almighty has done great things for me:
holy is his Name.
He has mercy on those who fear him
in every generation.

He has shown the strength of his arm,
he has scattered the proud in their conceit.
He has cast down the mighty from their thrones,
and has lifted up the lowly.
He has filled the hungry with good things,
and has sent the rich away empty.

He has come to the help of his servant Israel
for he has remembered his promise of mercy,
the promise he made to our fathers,
to Abraham and his children for ever.

Glory be to the Father ... (Lk 1:46-55)

Silent intercession is made for the following intentions:
For the unity of the Church ...
For all who work in public service ...
For the hungry and the destitute ...

During the Lord's Prayer the hands may be opened and
extended.

Our Father, who art in heaven,
hallowed be thy name.
Thy kingdom come.
Thy will be done on earth as it is in heaven.
Give us this day our daily bread,
and forgive us our trespasses
as we forgive those who trespass against us,
and lead us not into temptation,
but deliver us from evil.

Concluding Prayer

Father,
we thank you for showing us your mercy today;
may that mercy extend to all those
whom you entrust to our prayer;
and may it bring your peace to all people,
through Jesus Christ, our Lord. Amen.

The Sign of the Cross is made as the Blessing is said.

May Christ, the only Son of God, bless and help us.
Amen.

To the holy and undivided Trinity,
to the Father of all good gifts,
to the humanity of our Lord Jesus Christ, crucified and risen,
be all praise, honour and adoration
at this time and forevermore.

May the souls of the faithful departed through the mercy
of God rest in peace. Amen.

Week 2 Wednesday Morning: Lauds

The Sign of the Cross is traced on the lips while the opening
verse is said.

O Lord, open my lips.
And my mouth shall praise your name.

Glory be to the Father, and to the Son, and to the Holy
Spirit: as it was in the beginning, is now, and ever shall be,
world without end. Amen. (Alleluia.)

A candle may be lit in front of a Cross, a Bible, an icon or
a statue during the invocation of the light.
Now that I have risen from sleep,
I thank you, Lord of creation,
for keeping me safe throughout the night!
I bless you for the morning light and cry to you in adoration:
Holy, Holy, Holy are you, O Lord!
Have mercy on me and on the whole world!

A deep bow or other gesture of reverence may be made
while the following psalm verses are said:

Come, ring out our joy to the Lord;
hail the rock who saves us.

O that today you would listen to God's voice!
'Harden not your hearts'.

Glory be to the Father... (Ps 95:1, 7b, 8a)

Psalm

Have mercy on me, God, have mercy
for in you my soul has taken refuge.
In the shadow of your wings I take refuge
till the storms of destruction pass by.

I call to you, God the Most High,
to you who have always been my help.
May you send from heaven and save me
and shame those who assail me.
O God, send your truth and your love.

My heart is ready, O God, my heart is ready.
I will sing, I will sing your praise.
Awake, my soul; awake lyre and harp,
I will awake the dawn.

I will thank you, Lord, among the peoples,
among the nations I will praise you
for your love reaches to the heavens
and your truth to the skies.

O God, arise above the heavens;
may your glory shine on earth!

Glory be to the Father ... (Ps 57:1-4, 8-12)

Psalm Prayer
Tender God,
gentle protector in time of trouble,
pierce the gloom of despair
and give us, with all your people,
the song of freedom and the shout of praise;
in Jesus Christ our Lord. Amen.

Canticle
Surely God is my salvation;
I will trust, and will not be afraid,
for the Lord God is my strength and my might;
he has become my salvation.

With joy you will draw water from the wells of salvation.
Give thanks to the Lord, call on his name;
make known his deeds among the nations;
proclaim that his name is exalted.

Sing praises to the Lord, for he has done gloriously;
let this be known in all the earth.
Shout aloud and sing for joy, O royal Zion,
for great in your midst is the Holy One of Israel.

Glory be to the Father ... (Is 12:2-6)

Psalm of Praise
(Alleluia!)
Praise the Lord from the heavens,
praise God in the heights.
Praise God, all you angels,
praise him, all you hosts.

Praise God, sun and moon,
praise him, shining stars.
Praise God, highest heavens
and the waters above the heavens.

Let them praise the name of the Lord.
The Lord commanded: they were made.
God fixed them forever,
gave a law which shall not pass away.

God exalts the strength of the people,
is the praise of all the saints,
of the sons and daughters of Israel,
of the people to whom he comes close.
(Alleluia!)

Glory be to the Father ... (Ps 148:1-6, 14)

Psalm Prayer
O glorious God,
your whole creation sings your marvellous work;
may heaven's praise so echo in our hearts
that we may be good stewards of the earth;
through Jesus Christ our Lord. Amen.

Scripture reading

You are no longer strangers and aliens, but you are citizens
with the saints and also members of the household of
God, built upon the foundation of the apostles and
prophets, with Christ Jesus himself as the cornerstone. In
him the whole structure is joined together and grows into
a holy temple in the Lord; in whom you also are built
together spiritually into a dwelling-place for God.
(Eph 2:19-22)

The reading is followed by a pause for silent reflection.

The Sign of the Cross is made at the beginning of the
Gospel Canticle.

Gospel Canticle – The Benedictus

Blessed be the Lord, the God of Israel;
he has come to his people and set them free.
He has raised up for us a mighty saviour,
born of the house of his servant David.

Through his holy prophets he promised of old
that he would save us from our enemies,
from the hands of all who hate us.
He promised to show mercy to our fathers
and to remember his holy covenant.

This was the oath he swore to our father Abraham:
to set us free from the hands of our enemies,
free to worship him without fear,
holy and righteous in his sight all the days of our life.

You, my child, shall be called the prophet of the Most High
for you will go before the Lord to prepare his way,
to give his people knowledge of salvation
by forgiving them their sins.

In the tender compassion of our God
the dawn from on high shall break upon us,
to shine on those who dwell in darkness
and the shadow of death,
and to guide our feet on the road of peace.

Glory be to the Father … (Lk 1:68-79)

Silent thanksgiving is made for the following:
For all human deeds of kindness and compassion …
For the action of the Holy Spirit in the world …
For the grace and power of the sacraments …

During the Lord's Prayer the hands may be opened and
extended.

Our Father, who art in heaven,
hallowed be thy name.
Thy kingdom come.
Thy will be done on earth as it is in heaven.
Give us this day our daily bread,
and forgive us our trespasses
as we forgive those who trespass against us,
and lead us not into temptation,
but deliver us from evil.

Concluding Prayer
Father almighty,
you revealed to us that you are light.
Help us to live our lives in your radiance
and so be in fellowship with one another.
We ask this through Jesus Christ, our Lord. Amen.

The Sign of the Cross is made as the Blessing is said.

May God light the fire of his love in our hearts. Amen.

To the holy and undivided Trinity,
to the Father of all good gifts,
to the humanity of our Lord Jesus Christ, crucified and risen,
be all praise, honour and adoration
at this time and forevermore.

May the souls of the faithful departed through the mercy
of God rest in peace. Amen.

Week 2 Wednesday Evening: Vespers

The Sign of the Cross is made while the opening verse is said.

O God, come to my assistance.
O Lord, make haste to help me.

Glory be to the Father, and to the Son, and to the Holy Spirit: as it was in the beginning, is now, and ever shall be, world without end. Amen. (Alleluia.)

A candle may be lit in front of a Cross, a Bible, an icon or a statue during the thanksgiving for the light.

Now that the day has come to a close,
I thank you, Lord of creation,
for keeping me safe throughout this day!
I bless you for the evening light and cry to you in adoration:
Holy, Holy, Holy are you, O Lord!
Have mercy on me and on the whole world!

Incense may be burned while the following psalm verses are said:

Let my prayer arise before you like incense,
the raising of my hands like an evening sacrifice.

I have called to you, Lord; hasten to help me!
Hear my prayer when I cry to you!

Glory be to the Father… (Ps 141:2, 1)

Psalm

Lord, listen to my prayer,
turn your ear to my appeal.
You are faithful, you are just; give answer.
Do not call your servant to judgement
for no one is just in your sight.

The enemy pursues my soul;
has crushed my life to the ground;
has made me dwell in darkness
like the dead, long forgotten.
Therefore my spirit fails;
my heart is numb within me.

I remember the days that are past;
I ponder all your works.
I muse on what your hand has wrought
and to you I stretch out my hands.
Like a parched land my soul thirsts for you.

Lord, make haste and answer;
For my spirit fails within me.
Do not hide your face
lest I become like those in the grave.

In the morning let me know your love
for I put my trust in you.
Make me know the way I should walk;
to you I lift up my soul.

Glory be to the Father ... (Ps 143:1-8)

Psalm Prayer

Jesus, our companion,
when we are driven to despair,
help us, through the friends and strangers
we encounter on our path,
to know you as our refuge,
our way, our truth and our life. Amen.

Canticle

Great and amazing are your deeds,
Lord God the Almighty!
Just and true are your ways,
King of the nations!

Lord, who will not fear and glorify your name?
For you alone are holy.
All nations will come and worship before you,
for your judgements have been revealed.

Glory be to the Father ... (Rev 15:3-4)

Psalm of Praise

(Alleluia!)
O praise the Lord, Jerusalem!
Zion, praise your God!

God has strengthened the bars of your gates,
and has blessed the children within you;
has established peace on your borders,
and feeds you with finest wheat.

God sends out word to the earth

and swiftly runs the command.
God showers down snow white as wool,
and scatters hoarfrost like ashes.

God makes his word known to Jacob,
to Israel his laws and decrees.
God has not dealt thus with others nations;
has not taught them divine decrees.
(Alleluia!)

Glory be to the Father ... (Ps 147:12-16, 19-20)

Psalm Prayer
Compassionate God,
as you know each star you have created,
so you know the secrets of every heart;
in your loving mercy bring to your table
all who are fearful and broken,
all who are wounded and needy,
that our hungers may be satisfied in the city of your peace;
through Christ who is our peace. Amen.

Scripture reading

Blessed be the God and Father of our Lord Jesus Christ,
the Father of mercies and the God of all consolation, who
consoles us in all our affliction, so that we may be able to
console those who are in any affliction with the consolation with which we ourselves are consoled by God. For
just as the sufferings of Christ are abundant for us, so also
our consolation is abundant through Christ. (2 Cor 1:3-5)

The reading is followed by a pause for silent reflection.

The Sign of the Cross is made at the beginning of the
Gospel Canticle. Incense may be burned.

Gospel Canticle – The Magnificat

My soul proclaims the greatness of the Lord,
my spirit rejoices in God my Saviour;
for he has looked with favour on his lowly servant,
and from this day all generations will call me blessed.

The Almighty has done great things for me:
holy is his Name.
He has mercy on those who fear him
in every generation.

He has shown the strength of his arm,
he has scattered the proud in their conceit.
He has cast down the mighty from their thrones,
and has lifted up the lowly.
He has filled the hungry with good things,
and has sent the rich away empty.

He has come to the help of his servant Israel
for he has remembered his promise of mercy,
the promise he made to our fathers,
to Abraham and his children for ever.

Glory be to the Father … (Lk 1:46-55)

Silent intercession is made for the following intentions:
For those who struggle to believe …
For those who work in agriculture and food production …
For those who mourn …

During the Lord's Prayer the hands may be opened and
extended.

Our Father, who art in heaven,
hallowed be thy name.
Thy kingdom come.
Thy will be done on earth as it is in heaven.
Give us this day our daily bread,
and forgive us our trespasses
as we forgive those who trespass against us,
and lead us not into temptation,
but deliver us from evil.

Concluding Prayer

It is for you that we live, Lord our God,
and to you we have consecrated this day;
perfect and purify our offering,
so that our prayer of thanksgiving may rise to you,
in Jesus, your Son, our Lord. Amen.

The Sign of the Cross is made as the Blessing is said.

May God light the fire of his love in our hearts. Amen.

To the holy and undivided Trinity,
to the Father of all good gifts,
to the humanity of our Lord Jesus Christ, crucified and risen,
be all praise, honour and adoration
at this time and forevermore.

May the souls of the faithful departed through the mercy
of God rest in peace. Amen.

Week 2 Thursday Morning: Lauds

The Sign of the Cross is traced on the lips while the opening
verse is said.

O Lord, open my lips.
And my mouth shall praise your name.

Glory be to the Father, and to the Son, and to the Holy
Spirit: as it was in the beginning, is now, and ever shall be,
world without end. Amen. (Alleluia.)

A candle may be lit in front of a Cross, a Bible, an icon or
a statue during the invocation of the light.
Now that I have risen from sleep,
I thank you, Lord of creation,
for keeping me safe throughout the night!
I bless you for the morning light and cry to you in adoration:
Holy, Holy, Holy are you, O Lord!
Have mercy on me and on the whole world!

A deep bow or other gesture of reverence may be made
while the following psalm verses are said:

Come, ring out our joy to the Lord;
hail the rock who saves us.

O that today you would listen to God's voice!
'Harden not your hearts'.

Glory be to the Father… (Ps 95:1, 7b, 8a)

Psalm

Cry out with joy to the Lord, all the earth.
Serve the Lord with gladness.
Come before God, singing for joy.

Know that the Lord is God,
Our Maker, to whom we belong.
We are God's people, sheep of the flock.

Enter the gates with thanksgiving,
God's courts with songs of praise.
Give thanks to God and bless his name.

Indeed, how good is the Lord,
whose merciful love is eternal;
whose faithfulness lasts forever.

Glory be to the Father … (Ps 100)

Psalm Prayer

O Christ, door of the sheepfold,
may we enter your gates with praise
and go from your courts to serve you
in the poor, the lost and the wandering,
this day and all our days. Amen.

Canticle

O God of my ancestors and Lord of mercy,
who have made all things by your word,
give me the wisdom that sits by your throne,
and do not reject me from among your servants.

With you is wisdom, she who knows your works
and was present when you made the world;
she understands what is pleasing in your sight
and what is right according to your commandments.

Send her forth from the holy heavens,
and from the throne of your glory send her,
that she may labour at my side,
and that I may learn what is pleasing to you.

For she knows and understands all things,
and she will guide me wisely in my actions
and guard me with her glory.

Glory be to the Father … (Wis 9:1, 4, 9-11)

Psalm of Praise

(Alleluia!)
Praise God in his holy place,
Sing praise in the mighty heavens.
Sing praise for God's powerful deeds,
Praise God's surpassing greatness.

Sing praise with sound of trumpet,
Sing praise with lute and harp.
Sing praise with timbrel and dance,
Sing praise with strings and pipes.

Sing praise with resounding cymbals,
Sing praise with clashing of cymbals.
Let everything that lives and that breathes
give praise to the Lord. (Alleluia!)

Glory be to the Father … (Ps 150)

Psalm Prayer
God of life and love,
whose Son was victorious over sin and death,
make us alive with his life,
that the whole world may resound with your praise;
through Jesus Christ our Lord. Amen.

Scripture reading
Where, O death, is your victory? Where, O death, is your
sting? The sting of death is sin, and the power of sin is the
law. But thanks be to God, who gives us the victory
through our Lord Jesus Christ. (1 Cor 15:55-57)

The reading is followed by a pause for silent reflection.

The Sign of the Cross is made at the beginning of the
Gospel Canticle.

Gospel Canticle – The Benedictus
Blessed be the Lord, the God of Israel;
he has come to his people and set them free.
He has raised up for us a mighty saviour,
born of the house of his servant David.

Through his holy prophets he promised of old
that he would save us from our enemies,
from the hands of all who hate us.
He promised to show mercy to our fathers
and to remember his holy covenant.

This was the oath he swore to our father Abraham:
to set us free from the hands of our enemies,

free to worship him without fear,
holy and righteous in his sight all the days of our life.

You, my child, shall be called the prophet of the Most High
for you will go before the Lord to prepare his way,
to give his people knowledge of salvation
by forgiving them their sins.

In the tender compassion of our God
the dawn from on high shall break upon us,
to shine on those who dwell in darkness
and the shadow of death,
and to guide our feet on the road of peace.

Glory be to the Father ... (Lk 1:68-79)

Silent thanksgiving is made for the following:
For the example of holy lives ...
For signs of the coming of the Reign of God ...
For the communion of saints ...

During the Lord's Prayer the hands may be opened and extended.

Our Father, who art in heaven,
hallowed be thy name.
Thy kingdom come.
Thy will be done on earth as it is in heaven.
Give us this day our daily bread,
and forgive us our trespasses
as we forgive those who trespass against us,
and lead us not into temptation,
but deliver us from evil.

Concluding Prayer
God, our Father,
when you gave us your Son,
your light came into the world.
May we welcome him in our lives,
and thus be a light for our brothers and sisters.
We ask this through Jesus Christ, our Lord. Amen.

The Sign of the Cross is made as the Blessing is said.

May God be merciful to us and bless us. Amen.

To the holy and undivided Trinity,
to the Father of all good gifts,
to the humanity of our Lord Jesus Christ, crucified and risen,
be all praise, honour and adoration
at this time and forevermore.

May the souls of the faithful departed through the mercy
of God rest in peace. Amen.

Week 2 Thursday Evening: Vespers

The Sign of the Cross is made while the opening verse is said.

O God, come to my assistance.
O Lord, make haste to help me.

Glory be to the Father, and to the Son, and to the Holy Spirit: as it was in the beginning, is now, and ever shall be, world without end. Amen. (Alleluia.)

A candle may be lit in front of a Cross, a Bible, an icon or a statue during the thanksgiving for the light.

Now that the day has come to a close,
I thank you, Lord of creation,
for keeping me safe throughout this day!
I bless you for the evening light and cry to you in adoration:
Holy, Holy, Holy are you, O Lord!
Have mercy on me and on the whole world!

Incense may be burned while the following psalm verses are said:

Let my prayer arise before you like incense,
the raising of my hands like an evening sacrifice.

I have called to you, Lord; hasten to help me!
Hear my prayer when I cry to you!

Glory be to the Father... (Ps 141:2, 1)

Psalm

I thank you for the wonder of my being,
for the wonders of all your creation.
Already you knew my soul,
my body held no secret from you
when I was being fashioned in secret
and moulded in the depths of the earth.

Your eyes saw all my actions,
they were all of them written in your book;
every one of my days was decreed
before one of them came into being.

To me, how mysterious your thoughts,
the sum of them not to be numbered!
If I count them, they are more than the sand;
to finish, I must be eternal, like you.

O search me, God, and know my heart.
O test me and know my thoughts.
See that I follow not the wrong path
and lead me in the path of life eternal.

Glory be to the Father … (Ps 139:14-18, 23-24)

Psalm Prayer

Creator God,
may every breath we take be for your glory,
may every footstep show you as our way,
that, trusting in your presence in this world,
we may, beyond this life, still be with you
where you are alive and reign
for ever and ever. Amen.

Canticle

Give thanks to the Father,
who has enabled you to share
in the inheritance of the saints in the light.

He has rescued us from the power of darkness
and transferred us into the kingdom of his beloved Son,
in whom we have redemption,
the forgiveness of sins.

He is the image of the invisible God,
the firstborn of all creation;
for in him all things in heaven and on earth were created,
things visible and invisible.

All things have been created
through him and for him.
He himself is before all things,
and in him all things hold together.

He is the head of the body, the church;
he is the beginning,
the firstborn from the dead,
so that he might come to have first place in everything.

For in him all the fullness of God was pleased to dwell,
and through him God was pleased
to reconcile to himself all things,
whether on earth or in heaven,
by making peace through the blood of his cross.

Glory be to the Father ... (Col 1:12-20)

Psalm of Praise
(Alleluia!)
O praise the Lord, Jerusalem!
Zion, praise your God!

God has strengthened the bars of your gates,
and has blessed the children within you;
has established peace on your borders,
and feeds you with finest wheat.

God sends out word to the earth
and swiftly runs the command.
God showers down snow white as wool,
and scatters hoarfrost like ashes.

God makes his word known to Jacob,
to Israel his laws and decrees.
God has not dealt thus with others nations;
has not taught them divine decrees.
(Alleluia!)

Glory be to the Father ... (Ps 147:12-16, 19-20)

Psalm Prayer

Compassionate God,
as you know each star you have created,
so you know the secrets of every heart;
in your loving mercy bring to your table
all who are fearful and broken,
all who are wounded and needy,
that our hungers may be satisfied in the city of your peace;
through Christ who is our peace. Amen.

Scripture reading

What good is it, my brothers and sisters, if you say you
have faith but do not have works? Can faith save you? So
faith by itself, if it has no works, is dead. Show me your
faith without works, and I by my works will show you
my faith. (James 2:14, 17, 18b)

The reading is followed by a pause for silent reflection.

The Sign of the Cross is made at the beginning of the
Gospel Canticle. Incense may be burned.

Gospel Canticle – The Magnificat

My soul proclaims the greatness of the Lord,
my spirit rejoices in God my Saviour;
for he has looked with favour on his lowly servant,
and from this day all generations will call me blessed.

The Almighty has done great things for me:
holy is his Name.
He has mercy on those who fear him
in every generation.

He has shown the strength of his arm,
he has scattered the proud in their conceit.
He has cast down the mighty from their thrones,
and has lifted up the lowly.
He has filled the hungry with good things,
and has sent the rich away empty.

He has come to the help of his servant Israel
for he has remembered his promise of mercy,
the promise he made to our fathers,
to Abraham and his children for ever.

Glory be to the Father … (Lk 1:46-55)

Silent intercession is made for the following intentions:
For all preachers and evangelists …
For those who work to support families and communities …
For refugees and all displaced people …

During the Lord's Prayer the hands may be opened and
extended.

Our Father, who art in heaven,
hallowed be thy name.
Thy kingdom come.
Thy will be done on earth as it is in heaven.
Give us this day our daily bread,
and forgive us our trespasses
as we forgive those who trespass against us,
and lead us not into temptation,
but deliver us from evil.

Concluding Prayer

Lord God, ever faithful,
see us gathered before you
as the day draws to a close;
confirm our hearts in your love,
and keep alive in us
the memory of your goodness and kindness,
which have appeared in Jesus Christ, our Lord. Amen.

The Sign of the Cross is made as the Blessing is said.

May God be merciful to us and bless us. Amen.

To the holy and undivided Trinity,
to the Father of all good gifts,
to the humanity of our Lord Jesus Christ, crucified and risen,
be all praise, honour and adoration
at this time and forevermore.

May the souls of the faithful departed through the mercy
of God rest in peace. Amen.

Week 2 Friday Morning: Lauds

O Lord, open my lips.
And my mouth shall praise your name.

Glory be to the Father, and to the Son, and to the Holy Spirit: as it was in the beginning, is now, and ever shall be, world without end. Amen. (Alleluia.)

A candle may be lit in front of a Cross, a Bible, an icon or a statue during the invocation of the light.
Now that I have risen from sleep,
I thank you, Lord of creation,
for keeping me safe throughout the night!
I bless you for the morning light and cry to you in adoration:
Holy, Holy, Holy are you, O Lord!
Have mercy on me and on the whole world!

A deep bow or other gesture of reverence may be made while the following psalm verses are said:

Come, ring out our joy to the Lord;
hail the rock who saves us.

O that today you would listen to God's voice!
'Harden not your hearts'.

Glory be to the Father… (Ps 95:1, 7b, 8a)

Psalm

A pure heart create for me, O God,
put a steadfast spirit within me.
Do not cast me away from your presence,
nor deprive me of your holy spirit.

Give me again the joy of your help;
with a spirit of fervour sustain me,
that I may teach transgressors your ways
and sinners may return to you.

O rescue me, God, my helper,
and my tongue shall ring out your goodness.
O Lord, open my lips
and my mouth shall declare your praise.

For in sacrifice you take no delight,
burnt offering from me you would refuse;
my sacrifice, a contrite spirit,
a humbled, contrite heart you will not spurn.

Glory be to the Father … (Ps 51:12-19)

Psalm Prayer

Take away, good Lord, the sin that corrupts us;
give us the sorrow that heals and the joy that praises
and restore by grace your own image within us,
that we may take our place among your people;
in Jesus Christ our Lord. Amen.

Canticle

Hear, you who are far away, what I have done;
and you who are near, acknowledge my might.
The sinners in Zion are afraid;
trembling has seized the godless:

'Who among us can live with the devouring fire?
Who among us can live with everlasting flames?'
Those who walk righteously and speak uprightly,
who despise the gain of oppression,

who wave away a bribe instead of accepting it,
who stop their ears from hearing of bloodshed
and shut their eyes from looking on evil,

they will live on the heights;
their refuge will be the fortresses of rocks;
their food will be supplied, their water assured.

Glory be to the Father … (Is 33:13-16)

Psalm of Praise
(Alleluia!)
Praise God in his holy place,
Sing praise in the mighty heavens.
Sing praise for God's powerful deeds,
Praise God's surpassing greatness.

Sing praise with sound of trumpet,
Sing praise with lute and harp.
Sing praise with timbrel and dance,
Sing praise with strings and pipes.

Sing praise with resounding cymbals,
Sing praise with clashing of cymbals.
Let everything that lives and that breathes
give praise to the Lord.
(Alleluia!)

Glory be to the Father ... (Ps 150)

Psalm Prayer
God of life and love,
whose Son was victorious over sin and death,
make us alive with his life,
that the whole world may resound with your praise;
through Jesus Christ our Lord. Amen.

Scripture reading
I have been crucified with Christ; and it is no longer I
who live, but it is Christ who lives in me. And the life I
now live in the flesh I live by faith in the Son of God, who
loved me and gave himself for me. (Gal 2:19b-20)

The reading is followed by a pause for silent reflection.

The Sign of the Cross is made at the beginning of the
Gospel Canticle.

Gospel Canticle – The Benedictus
Blessed be the Lord, the God of Israel;
he has come to his people and set them free.
He has raised up for us a mighty saviour,
born of the house of his servant David.

Through his holy prophets he promised of old
that he would save us from our enemies,
from the hands of all who hate us.
He promised to show mercy to our fathers
and to remember his holy covenant.

This was the oath he swore to our father Abraham:
to set us free from the hands of our enemies,
free to worship him without fear,
holy and righteous in his sight all the days of our life.

You, my child, shall be called the prophet of the Most High
for you will go before the Lord to prepare his way,
to give his people knowledge of salvation
by forgiving them their sins.

In the tender compassion of our God
the dawn from on high shall break upon us,
to shine on those who dwell in darkness
and the shadow of death,
and to guide our feet on the road of peace.

Glory be to the Father ... (Lk 1:68-79)

Silent thanksgiving is made for the following:
For Christ's humble example on the cross ...
For the assurance of the forgiveness of sin...
For the example of all who lay down their lives for others ...

During the Lord's Prayer the hands may be opened and extended.

Our Father, who art in heaven,
hallowed be thy name.
Thy kingdom come.
Thy will be done on earth as it is in heaven.
Give us this day our daily bread,
and forgive us our trespasses
as we forgive those who trespass against us,
and lead us not into temptation,
but deliver us from evil.

Concluding Prayer

Lord Jesus,
your food was to do the will of your Father.
Make us attentive this day to the call of the Spirit,
and give us the strength to respond in humility,
for you are our help, for ever and ever. Amen.

The Sign of the Cross is made as the Blessing is said.

May the King of Friday lead us into paradise. Amen.

To the holy and undivided Trinity,
to the Father of all good gifts,
to the humanity of our Lord Jesus Christ, crucified and risen,
be all praise, honour and adoration
at this time and forevermore.

May the souls of the faithful departed through the mercy
of God rest in peace. Amen.

Week 2 Friday Evening: Vespers

The Sign of the Cross is made while the opening verse is said.

O God, come to my assistance.
O Lord, make haste to help me.

Glory be to the Father, and to the Son, and to the Holy
Spirit: as it was in the beginning, is now, and ever shall be,
world without end. Amen. (Alleluia.)

*A candle may be lit in front of a Cross, a Bible, an icon or
a statue during the thanksgiving for the light.*

Now that the day has come to a close,
I thank you, Lord of creation,
for keeping me safe throughout this day!
I bless you for the evening light and cry to you in adoration:
Holy, Holy, Holy are you, O Lord!
Have mercy on me and on the whole world!

*Incense may be burned while the following psalm verses
are said:*

Let my prayer arise before you like incense,
the raising of my hands like an evening sacrifice.

I have called to you, Lord; hasten to help me!
Hear my prayer when I cry to you!

Glory be to the Father... (Ps 141:2, 1)

Psalm

In you, O Lord, I take refuge.
Let me never be put to shame.
In your justice, set me free,
hear me and speedily rescue me.

Be a rock of refuge for me,
a mighty stronghold to save me,
for you are my rock, my stronghold.
For your name's sake, lead me and guide me.

Release me from the snares they have hidden
for you are my refuge, Lord.
Into your hands I commend my spirit.
It is you who will redeem me, Lord.

O God of truth, you detest
those who worship false and empty gods.
As for me, I trust in the Lord;
let me be glad and rejoice in your love.

You who have seen my affliction
and taken heed of my soul's distress,
have not handed me over to the enemy,
but set my feet at large.

Glory be to the Father … (Ps 31:1-8)

Psalm Prayer

Lord Jesus Christ,
when scorn and shame besiege us
and hope is veiled in grief,
hold us in your wounded hands
and make your face shine on us again,
for you are our Lord and God. Amen.

Canticle

Though he was in the form of God,
Jesus did not regard equality with God
as something to be exploited,
but emptied himself, taking the form of a slave,
being born in human likeness.

And being found in human form,
he humbled himself
and became obedient to the point of death –
even death on a cross.

Therefore God also highly exalted him
and gave him the name that is above every name,
so that at the name of Jesus every knee should bend,
in heaven and on earth and under the earth,
and every tongue should confess that Jesus Christ is Lord,
to the glory of God the Father.

Glory be to the Father ... (Phil 2:6-11)

Psalm of Praise

(Alleluia!)

O praise the Lord, Jerusalem!

Zion, praise your God!

God has strengthened the bars of your gates,

and has blessed the children within you;

has established peace on your borders,

and feeds you with finest wheat.

God sends out word to the earth

and swiftly runs the command.

God showers down snow white as wool,

and scatters hoarfrost like ashes.

God makes his word known to Jacob,

to Israel his laws and decrees.

God has not dealt thus with others nations;

has not taught them divine decrees.

(Alleluia!)

Glory be to the Father … (Ps 147:12-16, 19-20)

Psalm Prayer

Compassionate God,

as you know each star you have created,

so you know the secrets of every heart;

in your loving mercy bring to your table

all who are fearful and broken,

all who are wounded and needy,

that our hungers may be satisfied in the city of your peace;

through Christ who is our peace. Amen.

Scripture reading

When Christ had offered for all time a single sacrifice for sins, 'he sat down at the right hand of God', and since then has been waiting 'until his enemies would be made a footstool for his feet.' For by a single offering he has perfected for all time those who are sanctified.
(Heb 10:12-14)

The reading is followed by a pause for silent reflection.

The Sign of the Cross is made at the beginning of the Gospel Canticle. Incense may be burned.

Gospel Canticle – The Magnificat

My soul proclaims the greatness of the Lord,
my spirit rejoices in God my Saviour;
for he has looked with favour on his lowly servant,
and from this day all generations will call me blessed.

The Almighty has done great things for me:
holy is his Name.
He has mercy on those who fear him
in every generation.

He has shown the strength of his arm,
he has scattered the proud in their conceit.
He has cast down the mighty from their thrones,
and has lifted up the lowly.
He has filled the hungry with good things,
and has sent the rich away empty.

He has come to the help of his servant Israel
for he has remembered his promise of mercy,
the promise he made to our fathers,
to Abraham and his children for ever.

Glory be to the Father ... (Lk 1:46-55)

Silent intercession is made for the following intentions:
For all who suffer because of their faith in Christ...
For all who are unjustly deprived of their liberty ...
For the faithful departed ...

During the Lord's Prayer the hands may be opened and
extended.

Our Father, who art in heaven,
hallowed be thy name.
Thy kingdom come.
Thy will be done on earth as it is in heaven.
Give us this day our daily bread,
and forgive us our trespasses
as we forgive those who trespass against us,
and lead us not into temptation,
but deliver us from evil.

Concluding Prayer

May the memory of your death on the cross, Lord Jesus,
confirm our hearts in faith and hope;
then we shall live together in your love,
waiting for your coming,
for you are our Saviour, for ever and ever. Amen.

The Sign of the Cross is made as the Blessing is said.

May the King of Friday lead us into paradise. Amen.

To the holy and undivided Trinity,
to the Father of all good gifts,
to the humanity of our Lord Jesus Christ, crucified and risen,
be all praise, honour and adoration
at this time and forevermore.

May the souls of the faithful departed through the mercy
of God rest in peace. Amen.

Week 2 Saturday Morning: Lauds

The Sign of the Cross is traced on the lips while the opening verse is said.

O Lord, open my lips.
And my mouth shall praise your name.

Glory be to the Father, and to the Son, and to the Holy Spirit: as it was in the beginning, is now, and ever shall be, world without end. Amen. (Alleluia.)

A candle may be lit in front of a Cross, a Bible, an icon or a statue during the invocation of the light.

Now that I have risen from sleep,
I thank you, Lord of creation,
for keeping me safe throughout the night!
I bless you for the morning light and cry to you in adoration:
Holy, Holy, Holy are you, O Lord!
Have mercy on me and on the whole world!

A deep bow or other gesture of reverence may be made while the following psalm verses are said:

Come, ring out our joy to the Lord;
hail the rock who saves us.

O that today you would listen to God's voice!
'Harden not your hearts'.

Glory be to the Father... (Ps 95:1, 7b, 8a)

Psalm

Preserve me, God, I take refuge in you.
I say to the Lord: 'You are my God.
My happiness lies in you alone.'

You have put into my heart a marvellous love
for the faithful ones who dwell in your land.
Those who choose other gods increase their sorrows.
Never will I offer their offerings of blood.
Never will I take their name upon my lips.

O Lord, it is you who are my portion and cup,
it is you yourself who are my prize.
The lot marked out for me is my delight,
welcome indeed the heritage that falls to me!

I will bless you, Lord, you give me counsel,
and even at night direct my heart.
I keep you, Lord, ever in my sight;
since you are my right hand, I shall stand firm.

And so my heart rejoices, my soul is glad;
even my body shall rest in safety.
For you will not leave my soul among the dead,
nor let your beloved know decay.

You will show me the path of life,
the fullness of joy in your presence,
at your right hand happiness for ever.

Glory be to the Father … (Ps 16)

Psalm Prayer

Give to us, Lord Christ,
the fullness of grace,
your presence and your very self,
for you are our portion and our delight,
now and for ever. Amen.

Canticle

I will sing to the Lord, for he has triumphed gloriously;
horse and rider he has thrown into the sea.
The Lord is my strength and my might,
and he has become my salvation;

this is my God, and I will praise him,
my father's God, and I will exalt him.
Your right hand, O Lord, glorious in power –
your right hand, O Lord, shattered the enemy.

In your steadfast love
you led the people whom you redeemed;
you guided them by your strength to your holy abode.
You brought them in and planted them
on the mountain of your own possession,
the place, O Lord, that you made your abode,
the sanctuary, O Lord, that your hands have established.

Glory be to the Father … (Ex 15:1b-2, 6, 13, 17)

Psalm of Praise
(Alleluia!)
Praise God in his holy place,
Sing praise in the mighty heavens.
Sing praise for God's powerful deeds,
Praise God's surpassing greatness.

Sing praise with sound of trumpet,
Sing praise with lute and harp.
Sing praise with timbrel and dance,
Sing praise with strings and pipes.

Sing praise with resounding cymbals,
Sing praise with clashing of cymbals.
Let everything that lives and that breathes
give praise to the Lord.
(Alleluia!)

Glory be to the Father ... (Ps 150)

Psalm Prayer
God of life and love,
whose Son was victorious over sin and death,
make us alive with his life,
that the whole world may resound with your praise;
through Jesus Christ our Lord. Amen.

Scripture reading

Rejoice greatly, O daughter Zion! Shout aloud, O daughter
Jerusalem! Lo, your king comes to you; triumphant and
victorious is he, humble and riding on a donkey, on a colt,
the foal of a donkey. (Zech 9:9)

The reading is followed by a pause for silent reflection.

The Sign of the Cross is made at the beginning of the
Gospel Canticle.

Gospel Canticle – The Benedictus

Blessed be the Lord, the God of Israel;
he has come to his people and set them free.
He has raised up for us a mighty saviour,
born of the house of his servant David.

Through his holy prophets he promised of old
that he would save us from our enemies,
from the hands of all who hate us.
He promised to show mercy to our fathers
and to remember his holy covenant.

This was the oath he swore to our father Abraham:
to set us free from the hands of our enemies,
free to worship him without fear,
holy and righteous in his sight all the days of our life.

You, my child, shall be called the prophet of the Most High
for you will go before the Lord to prepare his way,
to give his people knowledge of salvation
by forgiving them their sins.

In the tender compassion of our God
the dawn from on high shall break upon us,
to shine on those who dwell in darkness
and the shadow of death,
and to guide our feet on the road of peace.

Glory be to the Father … (Lk 1:68-79)

Silent thanksgiving is made for the following:
For the presence of Christ with us …
For Mary's example of fidelity …
For the gift of friendship …

During the Lord's Prayer the hands may be opened and
extended.

Our Father, who art in heaven,
hallowed be thy name.
Thy kingdom come.
Thy will be done on earth as it is in heaven.
Give us this day our daily bread,
and forgive us our trespasses
as we forgive those who trespass against us,
and lead us not into temptation,
but deliver us from evil.

Concluding Prayer

God our Father,
you chose Mary from the lowly among your people,
and her one desire was to be your handmaid.
Through her intercession,
grant us poverty of spirit,
and reveal to us the mysteries of your kingdom,
through Jesus, the Christ, our Lord. Amen.

The Sign of the Cross is made as the Blessing is said.

May the most holy Mother of God intercede for us with
the Lord. Amen.

To the holy and undivided Trinity,
to the Father of all good gifts,
to the humanity of our Lord Jesus Christ, crucified and risen,
be all praise, honour and adoration
at this time and forevermore.

May the souls of the faithful departed through the mercy
of God rest in peace. Amen.

Week 2 Saturday Evening: Vespers

The Sign of the Cross is made while the opening verse is said.

O God, come to my assistance.
O Lord, make haste to help me.

Glory be to the Father, and to the Son, and to the Holy Spirit: as it was in the beginning, is now, and ever shall be, world without end. Amen. (Alleluia.)

A candle may be lit in front of a Cross, a Bible, an icon or a statue during the thanksgiving for the light.

Now that the day has come to a close,
I thank you, Lord of creation,
for keeping me safe throughout this day!
I bless you for the evening light and cry to you in adoration:
Holy, Holy, Holy are you, O Lord!
Have mercy on me and on the whole world!

Incense may be burned while the following psalm verses are said:

Let my prayer arise before you like incense,
the raising of my hands like an evening sacrifice.

I have called to you, Lord; hasten to help me!
Hear my prayer when I cry to you!

Glory be to the Father... (Ps 141:2, 1)

Psalm

Praise, O servants of the Lord,
praise the name of the Lord!
May the name of the Lord be blessed
both now and for evermore!
From the rising of the sun to its setting
praised be the name of the Lord!

High above all nations is the Lord,
above the heavens God's glory.
Who is like the Lord, our God,
the one enthroned on high,
who stoops from the heights to look down,
to look down upon heaven and earth?

From the dust God lifts up the lowly,
from the dungheap God raises the poor
to set them in the company of rulers,
yes, with the rulers of the people.
To the childless wife God gives a home
and gladdens her heart with children.

Glory be to the Father … (Ps 113)

Psalm Prayer

From the rising of the sun to its setting
we praise your name, O Lord;
may your promise to raise the poor from the dust
and turn the fortunes of the needy upside down
be fulfilled in our time also,
as it was in your Son, Jesus Christ our Lord. Amen.

Canticle

You are worthy, our Lord and God,
to receive glory and honour and power,
for you created all things,
and by your will they existed and were created.

You are worthy to take the scroll
and to open its seals,
for you were slaughtered and by your blood
you ransomed for God
saints from every tribe and language and people and nation.

You have made them to be a kingdom
and priests serving our God,
and they will reign on earth.

Worthy is the Lamb that was slaughtered
to receive power and wealth
and wisdom and might
and honour and glory and blessing!

Glory be to the Father ... (Rev 4:11, 5:9, 10, 12)

Psalm of Praise

(Alleluia!)
O praise the Lord, Jerusalem!
Zion, praise your God!

God has strengthened the bars of your gates,
and has blessed the children within you;
has established peace on your borders,
and feeds you with finest wheat.

God sends out word to the earth
and swiftly runs the command.
God showers down snow white as wool,
and scatters hoarfrost like ashes.

God makes his word known to Jacob,
to Israel his laws and decrees.
God has not dealt thus with others nations;
has not taught them divine decrees.
(Alleluia!)

Glory be to the Father ... (Ps 147:12-16, 19-20)

Psalm Prayer
Compassionate God,
as you know each star you have created,
so you know the secrets of every heart;
in your loving mercy bring to your table
all who are fearful and broken,
all who are wounded and needy,
that our hungers may be satisfied in the city of your peace;
through Christ who is our peace. Amen.

Scripture reading
We do not live to ourselves, and we do not die to ourselves. If we live, we live to the Lord, and if we die, we
die to the Lord; so then, whether we live or whether we
die, we are the Lord's. For to this end Christ died and
lived again, so that he might be Lord of both the dead
and the living. (Rom 14:7-9)

The reading is followed by a pause for silent reflection.

The Sign of the Cross is made at the beginning of the Gospel Canticle. Incense may be burned.

Gospel Canticle – The Magnificat
My soul proclaims the greatness of the Lord,
my spirit rejoices in God my Saviour;
for he has looked with favour on his lowly servant,
and from this day all generations will call me blessed.

The Almighty has done great things for me:
holy is his Name.
He has mercy on those who fear him
in every generation.

He has shown the strength of his arm,
he has scattered the proud in their conceit.
He has cast down the mighty from their thrones,
and has lifted up the lowly.
He has filled the hungry with good things,
and has sent the rich away empty.

He has come to the help of his servant Israel
for he has remembered his promise of mercy,
the promise he made to our fathers,
to Abraham and his children for ever.

Glory be to the Father ... (Lk 1:46-55)

Silent intercession is made for the following intentions:
For the building-up of the Church …
For the outpouring of the Holy Spirit on the world …
For the coming of the kingdom …

During the Lord's Prayer the hands may be opened and extended.

Our Father, who art in heaven,
hallowed be thy name.
Thy kingdom come.
Thy will be done on earth as it is in heaven.
Give us this day our daily bread,
and forgive us our trespasses
as we forgive those who trespass against us,
and lead us not into temptation,
but deliver us from evil.

Concluding Prayer
God our Father,
when Jesus was dying for us
Mary his mother stood by his side,
in the darkness which covered the earth.
In the unending dawn of the resurrection,
may she stand as a sign of our sure hope,
that we will one day be with you,
that Light that will shine for ever and ever. Amen.

The Sign of the Cross is made as the Blessing is said.

Through the prayers of your most pure mother and of all your saints, Lord Jesus Christ, have mercy on us and save us. Amen.

To the holy and undivided Trinity,
to the Father of all good gifts,
to the humanity of our Lord Jesus Christ, crucified and risen,
be all praise, honour and adoration
at this time and forevermore.

May the souls of the faithful departed through the mercy of God rest in peace. Amen.

Saints and Seasons

Advent

The church's liturgical year begins with the season of Advent, which means arrival or coming. We recall the first coming of Christ (in the incarnation at Christmas) and anticipate his final coming (at the end of time). We celebrate with joy his daily coming in the time of the church, in word and sacrament. It is a season of hope and anticipation: purple vestments symbolise the yearning of the church and of all creation for the transforming light of Christ.

Alternative Psalm verses for after the invocation of light (Lauds) and after the thanksgiving for light (Vespers)
O shepherd of Israel, hear us,
shine forth from your cherubim throne.

O Lord, rouse up your might,
O Lord, come to our help.

Glory be to the Father ... (Ps 80:2a, c; 3b, c)

Concluding Prayer
Before 17 December the emphasis falls on the second coming:
Ever faithful God,
your prophets foretold the coming of the light.
In your name they promised
that the eyes of the blind would be opened.
We confidently await the coming of your Son,
and the day when he will gather all people
to live in your light, for ever and ever. Amen

Between 17 and 25 December, we prepare for the feast of
Christmas itself:
God, Lord of eternity,
your Son came to visit us in time.
Grant to each of us the heart of a child
which never ceases to marvel at your wonders,
so that once again this day
you may find us watching in hope.
We ask you this, because of your love for us,
God blessed for ever and ever. Amen.

Blessing

Through the long-awaited coming of your Son,
deliver us, O Lord, from our age-old bondage to sin. Amen.

Christmas

At Christmas we celebrate the mystery of Jesus Christ, the Word made flesh for our salvation. In the incarnate Lord, a child held in the arms of Mary, we see our God made visible and so are caught up in love for the invisible God. The joy of Christmas overflows into the feasts of the Epiphany and the Baptism of Christ: these proclaim that the message of salvation, radiating from the chosen people, has shone upon the whole human race. This Christmas joy is reflected in the white vestments and Christmas crib.

Alternative Psalm verses for after the invocation of light (Lauds) and after the thanksgiving for light (Vespers)
The Lord has made known his salvation;
has shown his justice to the nations.

All the ends of the earth have seen
the salvation of our God.

Glory be to the Father … (Ps 98:2, 3)

Concluding Prayer

Lord our God,
you sent your Son, the Light of the World,
into the darkness
which covered the earth and its peoples.
May the brightness of his rising
shine in the church,
so that the nations may walk towards the light,
Jesus, the Christ, our Lord. Amen.

Blessing

May the light of the new-born Christ
bring peace to the world
and may the Sun of Justice rise in our hearts. Amen.

Lent

Lent is the forty days of preparation for the celebration of Christ's saving death and resurrection at Easter. It is a time of purification in which Christians struggle to fulfill their baptismal promises, by dying to selfishness and living for Christ. It begins with Ash Wednesday, a reminder of our mortality, but ends in the celebration of undying life at Easter. St Benedict tells his monks that life should always have a Lenten character about it, because the Christian is always journeying from the old realm of sin and death to the light and love of God's kingdom. In Lent all alleluias are omitted.

Alternative Psalm verses for after the invocation of light (Lauds) and after the thanksgiving for light (Vespers)
O Lord, listen to my prayer
and let my cry for help reach you.

You will arise and have mercy on Zion:
for this is the time to have mercy,
yes, the appointed time has come.

Glory be to the Father … (Ps 102:1, 14)

Concluding Prayer

God our Father,
your will is that everyone be saved and no one be lost.
You draw us to yourself by prayer and penance.
Grant that we may so follow Christ in love
that our lives may help others
and our weakness never hinder them.
We make this prayer in his name,
Jesus, the Christ, our Lord. Amen.

Blessing

Bless us, O Lord, with pardon and peace,
that serving you with pure hearts and quiet minds,
we may come at last to the victory of Easter. Amen.

Holy Week

At the end of Lent we begin Holy Week with the commemoration of Christ's entry into Jerusalem on Palm Sunday. The church follows the path of Jesus from Gethsemane to Golgotha and the glory of the resurrection. During the three great days of the Paschal Triduum, (Holy Thursday, Good Friday and Easter Day) the events by which God saved us are celebrated: the gift of the Holy Eucharist, the agony in the garden, the passion of the Lord, his descent into hell and his resurrection from the dead. In the celebration of the great vigil on Easter night, the triumphant proclamation of undying hope is sounded: 'Christ is risen! He is truly risen!'

Alternative Psalm verses for after the invocation of light (Lauds) and after the thanksgiving for light (Vespers)

Christ was humbler yet,
even to accepting death, death on a cross.

God made the sinless one into sin,
so that in him,
we might become the righteousness of God.

Glory be to the Father … (Phil 2:8; 2 Cor 5:21)

Concluding Prayer

God of mercy,
your Son Jesus chose suffering and the cross
in place of the joy that was held out to him;
teach us to carry one another's burdens,
that we may die and rise again
to live in him who is our Saviour,
for ever and ever. Amen.

Blessing

May the glorious cross of the Son of God
protect us in life and in death
and lead us safely to our heavenly home. Amen.

Easter

The joy of the paschal vigil overflows into the great Fifty Days of the Easter season. Gold and white vestments are worn in church and alleluia is sung repeatedly. The season culminates in the return of Christ to the Father at the Ascension and their sending of the Holy Spirit at Pentecost. Both Holy Week and the Easter season however are not merely a historical remembrance of past events. Through the celebration of the liturgy, the Holy Spirit makes the glorified Lord Jesus present to the church, keeping alive his promise that he would be with us until the end of time. Easter is the centre of the life of grace through which we are adopted as God's children: Christ's victory over death is shared with us.

Alternative Psalm verses for after the invocation of light (Lauds) and after the thanksgiving for light (Vespers)
Christ is risen!
He is risen indeed!

O Christ, Wisdom, Word and Power of God!
Let us share in your eternal day,
which knows no evening. Alleluia!

Glory be to the Father …

Concluding Prayer

Lord our God, by the resurrection of your Son,
you have forever illumined the world.
Through the power of your Spirit,
grant that those who still sit in darkness
and in the shadow of death,
may be born anew,
and that your light may shine on them
for ever and ever. Amen.

Blessing

May the Light of Christ, rising in glory,
scatter the darkness of our hearts and minds. Alleluia!

Saints: Mary

Alternative Psalm verses for after the invocation of light
(Lauds) and after the thanksgiving for light (Vespers)
You are the glory of Jerusalem,
you are the joy of Israel,
you are the highest honour of our race!

The Lord, the Most High God,
has blessed you above all others,
O Sinless Virgin Mary.

Glory be to the Father …

Concluding Prayer
Lord our God,
You have wrought marvels in Mary, your lowly handmaid.
May our weakness and our poverty
ever manifest the power of your grace,
through Jesus, your Son, our Lord. Amen.

Blessing
Through the prayers of the most pure Mother of God,
O Saviour, save us. Amen.

Other Saints

Alternative Psalm verses for after the invocation of light
(Lauds) and after the thanksgiving for light (Vespers)

Ring out your joy to the Lord, O you just;
for praise is fitting for loyal hearts.

They are happy whose God is the Lord,
the people he has chosen as his own.

Glory be to the Father … (Ps 33:1, 12)

Concluding Prayer

We give you thanks, our Lord and God,
for Saint(s) *N,*
and the unnumbered company of witnesses
whose prayer and love surround us.
May they, although unseen,
sustain and strengthen us
on our journey towards your light,
Jesus Christ, our Lord. Amen.

Blessing

Let the cries of your servants come to you, O Lord,
and through the prayers of Saints(s) *N*
and of all your holy ones,
grant peace and salvation to your people. Amen.

For the Dead

Alternative Psalm verses for after the invocation of light
(Lauds) and after the thanksgiving for light (Vespers)

Eternal rest grant unto them, O Lord,
and let perpetual light shine upon them!

From the power of death,
deliver their souls, O Lord!

Glory be to the Father …

Concluding Prayer
Lord our God,
you have created us anew
and your Spirit dwells in our mortal bodies.
In your presence
we remember all those who have died (especially *N*).
May your Spirit of life
transform them into the likeness of your Son,
who conquered death
for ever and ever. Amen.

Blessing
Listen to our prayers, Lord Jesus Christ,
and have mercy on us:
grant to the faithful departed
the joyful vision of your glory. Amen

Prayer Stops

Mid-Morning: Terce

An appeal for the Holy Spirit of Pentecost

The Sign of the Cross is made while the opening verse is said.

O God, come to my assistance.
O Lord, make haste to help me.

Glory be to the Father, and to the Son, and to the Holy Spirit: as it was in the beginning, is now, and ever shall be, world without end. Amen. (Alleluia.)

Psalm
To the Lord in the hour of my distress
I call and he answers me.
'O Lord, save my soul from lying lips,
from the tongue of the deceitful.'

What shall God pay you in return,
O treacherous tongue?
Arrows sharpened for war
and coals, red-hot, blazing.

Long enough have I been dwelling
with those who hate peace.
I am for peace, but when I speak,
they are for fighting.

Glory be to the Father ... (Ps 120)

Psalm Prayer
God of consolation,
look on us, pilgrims in a strange land;
preserve us from slander and deceit,
show us the truth
and give to our souls the peace of Christ. Amen.

Psalm
I lift up my eyes to the mountains;
from where shall come my help?
My help shall come from the Lord
who made heaven and earth.

May God never allow you to stumble!
Let your guard not sleep.
Behold, neither sleeping nor slumbering,
Israel's guard.

The Lord is your guard and your shade;
and stands at your right.
By day the sun shall not smite you
nor the moon in the night.

The Lord will guard you from evil,
and will guard your soul.
The Lord will guard your going and coming
both now and for ever.

Glory be to the Father … (Ps 121)

Psalm Prayer

Lord, ever watchful and faithful,
we look to you to be our defence
and we lift our hearts to know your help;
through Jesus Christ our Lord. Amen.

The psalms are followed by a pause for silent reflection.

Invocations

Blessed are you Lord God, who gave the gift of your Holy
Spirit to the apostles at this hour:
Glory to you, O Lord!

Blessed are you Lord Jesus Christ,
who sent us the Spirit of truth:
Glory to you, O Lord!

Blessed are you, Spirit of life who search the deep things
of God and reveal his love to us:
Glory to you, O Lord!

During the Lord's Prayer the hands may be opened and
extended.

Our Father, who art in heaven,
hallowed be thy name.
Thy kingdom come.
Thy will be done on earth as it is in heaven.
Give us this day our daily bread,
and forgive us our trespasses
as we forgive those who trespass against us,
and lead us not into temptation,
but deliver us from evil.

Concluding Prayer

All-holy Father,
at this hour when the Spirit came down on the apostles,
we ask you to help us live throughout this day
the love that they proclaimed,
through Jesus Christ our Lord. Amen.

The Sign of the Cross is made as the following is said.

May the grace of the Holy Spirit enlighten our hearts and
our senses. Amen.

Mid-day: Sext
Recalling the Passion of Jesus

The Sign of the Cross is made while the opening verse is said.

O God, come to my assistance.
O Lord, make haste to help me.

Glory be to the Father, and to the Son, and to the Holy Spirit: as it was in the beginning, is now, and ever shall be, world without end. Amen. (Alleluia.)

Psalm

I rejoiced when I heard them say:
'Let us go to God's house,'
And now our feet are standing
within your gates, O Jerusalem.

Jerusalem is built as a city
strongly compact.
It is there that the tribes go up,
the tribes of the Lord.

For Israel's law it is,
there to praise the Lord's name.
There were set the thrones of judgement
of the house of David.

For the peace of Jerusalem pray:
'Peace be to your homes!
May peace reign in your walls,
in your palaces, peace!'

For the love of my family and friends
I say: 'Peace upon you.'
For the love of the house of the Lord
I will ask for your good.

Glory be to the Father … (Ps 122)

Psalm Prayer

God of our pilgrimage,
bring us with joy to the eternal city
founded on the rock,
and give to our earthly cities
the peace that comes from above;
through Jesus Christ our Lord. Amen.

Psalm

To you have I lifted up my eyes,
you who dwell in the heavens;
my eyes like the eyes of slaves
on the hand of their lords.

Like the eyes of a servant
on the hand of her mistress,
so our eyes are on the Lord our God
till we are shown mercy.

Have mercy on us, Lord, have mercy.
We are filled with contempt.
Indeed all too full is our soul
with the scorn of the rich,
(the disdain of the proud).

Glory be to the Father ... (Ps 123)

Psalm Prayer
Sovereign God, enthroned in the heavens,
look upon us with your eyes of mercy,
as we look on you with humility and love,
and fill our souls with your peace
through Jesus Christ our Lord. Amen.

The psalms are followed by a pause for silent reflection.

Invocations
On the cross, O Christ, you opened your arms to us in love:
gather all people to yourself in unity and peace!

By the power of your cross, O Christ,
you have given us new life:
show your mercy to all who call upon you!

In the strength of your cross, O Christ,
you have filled the world with light:
we cry to you with joy and thanks!

During the Lord's Prayer the hands may be opened and extended.

Our Father, who art in heaven,
hallowed be thy name.
Thy kingdom come.
Thy will be done on earth as it is in heaven.
Give us this day our daily bread,
and forgive us our trespasses
as we forgive those who trespass against us,
and lead us not into temptation,
but deliver us from evil.

Concluding Prayer

Lord Jesus, Saviour of the world,
this is the hour when you were lifted up from the earth.
By looking on your cross
and seeing the depth of your love for us,
may we never again stray from you,
who reign with the Father for ever and ever. Amen.

The Sign of the Cross is made as the Blessing is said.

We adore you, O Christ, and we bless you, because by
your holy cross you have redeemed the world. Amen.

Afternoon: None

A remembrance of Christ's death

O God, come to my assistance.
O Lord, make haste to help me.

Glory be to the Father, and to the Son, and to the Holy
Spirit: as it was in the beginning, is now, and ever shall be,
world without end. Amen. (Alleluia.)

Psalm
'If the Lord had not been on our side,'
this is Israel's song.
'If the Lord had not been on our side
when they rose up against us,
then would they have swallowed us alive
when their anger was kindled.

Then would the waters have engulfed us,
the torrent gone over us;
over our head would have swept
the raging waters.'

Blessed be the Lord who did not give us
a prey to their teeth!
Our life, like a bird, has escaped
from the snare of the fowler.

Indeed the snare has been broken
and we have escaped.
Our help is in the name of the Lord,
who made heaven and earth.

Glory be to the Father … (Ps 124)

Psalm Prayer
O God, maker of heaven and earth,
you save us in the water of baptism
and by the suffering of your Son you set us free;
help us to put our trust in his victory
and to know the salvation won for us
by Jesus Christ our Lord. Amen.

Psalm
Those who put their trust in the Lord
are like Mount Zion, that cannot be shaken,
that stands for ever.

Jerusalem! The mountains surround her,
so the Lord surrounds his people
both now and for ever.

For the sceptre of the wicked shall not rest
over the land of the just
for fear that the hands of the just
should turn to evil.

Do good, Lord, to those who are good,
to the upright of heart;
but the crooked and those who do evil,
drive them away!

Glory be to the Father ... (Ps 125)

Psalm Prayer
God of power,
you are strong to save
and you never fail those who trust in you;
keep us under your protection
and spread abroad your reign of peace
through Jesus Christ our Lord. Amen.

The psalms are followed by a pause for silent reflection.

Invocations
At this hour, O Christ our Lord,
you suffered death upon the cross:
save us by your passion, O compassionate Saviour!

You were buried for us and knew the darkness of the
tomb:
Jesus, unquenchable light, raise us to life with you!

You descended to the dead, that your salvation might
reach to the ends of the earth:
rise in our hearts, O dayspring from on high!

During the Lord's Prayer the hands may be opened and
extended.

Our Father, who art in heaven,
hallowed be thy name.
Thy kingdom come.
Thy will be done on earth as it is in heaven.
Give us this day our daily bread,
and forgive us our trespasses
as we forgive those who trespass against us,
and lead us not into temptation,
but deliver us from evil.

Concluding Prayer

At the ninth hour, Lord Jesus,
you gave yourself into the hands of the Father.
May we welcome his will with love and fulfil it to the end,
as you have taught us,
who reign for ever and ever. Amen.

The Sign of the Cross is made as the following is said.

We venerate your cross, O Lord. We praise and glorify
your holy resurrection. Because of the wood of the tree,
joy has come into the whole world. Amen.

Night 1: Compline

I confess to almighty God,
and to you, my brothers and sisters,
that I have sinned through my own fault
in my thoughts and in my words,
in what I have done and in what I have failed to do;
and I ask Blessed Mary, ever virgin,
all the angels and saints,
and you, my brothers and sisters,
to pray for me to the Lord our God.

May almighty God have mercy on us,
forgive us our sins, and bring us to everlasting life. Amen.

O God, come to my assistance.
O Lord, make haste to help me.

Glory be to the Father, and to the Son, and to the Holy Spirit: as it was in the beginning, is now, and ever shall be, world without end. Amen. (Alleluia.)

Psalms

When I call, answer me, O God of justice;
from anguish you released me, have mercy and hear me!

You rebels, how long will your hearts be closed,
will you love what is futile and seek what is false?

It is the Lord who grants favours
to those who are merciful;
the Lord who hears me whenever I call.

Tremble; do not sin: ponder on your bed and be still.
Make justice your sacrifice and trust in the Lord.

'What can bring us happiness?' many say.
Lift up the light of your face on us, O Lord.

You have put into my heart a greater joy
than they have from abundance of corn and new wine.

I will lie down in peace and sleep comes at once
for you alone, Lord, make me dwell in safety.

Pause

O come, bless the Lord,
all you who serve the Lord,
who stand in the house of the Lord,
in the courts of the house of our God.
Lift up your hands to the holy place
and bless the Lord through the night.
May the Lord bless you from Zion,
God who made both heaven and earth.

Glory be to the Father ... (Ps 4 and Ps 134)

Scripture reading

They will see the Lord's face, and his name will be on
their foreheads. And there will be no more night; they
need no light of lamp or sun, for the Lord God will be
their light, and they will reign for ever and ever. (Rev 22:4-5)

The reading is followed by a pause for silent reflection.

The Sign of the Cross is made at the beginning of the
Gospel Canticle.

Gospel Canticle – The Nunc Dimittis
Save us Lord, while we are awake;
protect us while we sleep,
that we may keep watch with Christ,
and rest with him in peace.

At last, all powerful Master,
you give leave to your servant
to go in peace,
according to your promise.

For my eyes have seen your salvation
which you have prepared for all nations,
the light to enlighten the Gentiles
and give glory to Israel, your people.

Glory be to the Father ... (Lk 2:29-32)

Save us Lord, while we are awake;
protect us while we sleep,
that we may keep watch with Christ,
and rest with him in peace.

Concluding Prayer

Guard all your household, Lord,
through the dark night of faith,
and purify the hearts of those who wait on you,
until your kingdom dawns
with the rising of your Son,
Christ, the morning star. Amen.

The Sign of the Cross is made as the Blessing is said.

May the Lord grant us a quiet night and a perfect end.
Amen.

An antiphon in honour of Our Lady ends the day's
prayer.

Salve Regina mater misericordiæ,
vita, dulcedo et spes nostra, salve.
Ad te clamamus exsules filii Hevæ.
Ad te suspiramus gementes et flentes
in hac lacrimarum valle.
Eia ergo, advocata nostra,
illos tuos misericordes oculos ad nos converte.
Et Jesum, benedictum fructum ventris tui,
nobis post hoc exilium ostende.
O clemens, O pia, O dulcis Virgo Maria.

Hail, Holy Queen, Mother of Mercy!
Hail, our life, our sweetness, and our hope!
To thee do we cry, poor banished children of Eve;
to thee do we send up our sighs,
mourning and weeping in this valley of tears.
Turn, then, most gracious advocate,
thine eyes of mercy towards us;
and after this our exile
show unto us the blessed fruit of thy womb, Jesus;
O clement, O loving, O sweet Virgin Mary.

Night 2: Compline

An Examination of Conscience may conclude with the following penitential act:

Lord, we have sinned against you:
Lord, have mercy.

Lord, show us your mercy and love:
And grant us your salvation.

May almighty God have mercy on us,
forgive us our sins, and bring us to everlasting life. Amen.

The Sign of the Cross is made while the opening verse is said.

O God, come to my assistance.
O Lord, make haste to help me.

Glory be to the Father, and to the Son, and to the Holy Spirit: as it was in the beginning, is now, and ever shall be, world without end. Amen. (Alleluia.)

Psalm
Those who dwell in the shelter of the Most High
and abide in the shade of the Almighty
say to the Lord: 'My refuge,
my stronghold, my God in whom I trust!'

It is God who will free you from the snare
of the fowler who seeks to destroy you;
God will conceal you with his pinions,
and under his wings you will find refuge.

You will not fear the terror of the night
nor the arrow that flies by day,
nor the plague that prowls in the darkness
nor the scourge that lays waste at noon.

A thousand may fall at your side,
ten thousand fall at your right,
you, it will never approach;
God's faithfulness is buckler and shield.

Your eyes have only to look
to see how the wicked are repaid,
you who have said: 'Lord, my refuge!'
and have made the Most High your dwelling.

Upon you no evil shall fall,
No plague approach where you dwell.
For you God has commanded the angels,
to keep you in all your ways.

They shall bear you upon their hands
lest you strike your foot against a stone.
On the lion and the viper you will tread
and trample the young lion and the dragon.

You set your love on me so I will save you,
protect you for you know my name.
When you call I shall answer: 'I am with you,'
I will save you in distress and give you glory.

With length of days I will content you;
I shall let you see my saving power.

Glory be to the Father … (Ps 91)

Scripture reading
May the God of peace himself sanctify you entirely; and
may your spirit and soul and body be kept sound and
blameless at the coming of our Lord Jesus Christ.
(1 Thess 5:23)

The reading is followed by a pause for silent reflection.

The Sign of the Cross is made at the beginning of the
Gospel Canticle.

Gospel Canticle – The Nunc Dimittis
Save us Lord, while we are awake;
protect us while we sleep,
that we may keep watch with Christ,
and rest with him in peace.

At last, all powerful Master,
you give leave to your servant
to go in peace,
according to your promise.

For my eyes have seen your salvation
which you have prepared for all nations,
the light to enlighten the Gentiles
and give glory to Israel, your people.

Glory be to the Father … (Lk 2:29-32)

Save us Lord, while we are awake;
protect us while we sleep,
that we may keep watch with Christ,
and rest with him in peace.

Concluding Prayer
Bless our sleep, Lord God,
and make it a continuation of our trustful prayer;
so that even while we rest,
our hearts may remain watchful,
through Jesus, the Christ, our Lord. Amen.

The Sign of the Cross is made as the Blessing is said.

May the Almighty and Merciful Lord bless and protect us,
the Father, the Son, and the Holy Spirit. Amen.

An antiphon in honour of Our Lady ends the day's
prayer.

Sub tuum præsidium confugimus,
Sancta Dei Genetrix;
nostras deprecationes ne despicias
in necessitatibus,
sed a periculis cunctis libera nos semper,
Virgo gloriosa et benedicta.

We fly to your protection,
O holy Mother of God.
Despise not our petitions in our need,
but free us from every danger,
O blessed and glorious Virgin.